FACTFINDER GUIDE
WARRIORS

FACTFINDER GUIDE
WARRIORS

Ian Westwell
Nick Grant

PRC

This edition first published in 1999 by
PRC Publishing Ltd,
Kiln House, 210 New Kings Road, London
SW6 4NZ

© 1999 PRC Publishing Ltd

All rights reserved. No part of this publication may be reproduced, stored in a retrieval system, or transmitted in any form or by any means, electronic, mechanical, photocopying, recording, or otherwise, without the prior written permission of the Publisher and copyright holders.

ISBN 1 85648 527 7

Printed and bound in China

PAGE 2: US MARINES PRACTICE BUSH TACTICS IN THE JUNGLES OF THE SOUTH PACIFIC DURING WORLD WAR II.

PAGE 3: A ROMAN LEGIONNAIRE CIRCA 157-86 BC.

CONTENTS

INTRODUCTION	6
Sumerian infantry	18
Egyptian charioteer	20
Assyrian archer	22
Persian immortal	24
Spartan hoplite	26
Carthaginian cavalry	28
Roman legionnaire	30
Byzantine cavalry	32
Arthurian cavalryman	34
Arab cavalryman	36
Frankish cavalryman	38
Viking hersir	40
Norman knight	42
Crusader knight	44
Mongol cavalryman	46
English longbowman	48
French knight	50
Hussite infantry	52
Swiss pikeman	54
German reiter	56
Spanish infantry	58
Ottoman janissary	60
Samurai warrior	62
Royalist cavalryman	64
Cromwellian muskeeteer	66
American ranger	68
Highland clansman	70
Prussian grenadier	72
Colonial minuteman	74
Continental infantry	76
Grenadier of the imperial guard	78
Wellington's Army	80
US infantry	82
Union Soldier	84
Confederate Soldier	86
US Cavalryman	88
Apache Brave	90
Zulu Impi Warrior	92
Boer Sharpshooter	94
World War I	**96**
German Stormtrooper	98
French Poilu	100
British Tommy	102
U.S. Doughboy	104
German Airman	106
Royal Flying Corps Airman	108
British Tank Crew	110
World War II	**112**
Waffen-SS Soldier	114
Afrikakorps Soldier	116
Japanese Infantryman	118
British Paratrooper	120
U.S. Paratrooper	122
US Infantryman	124
B-17 Crew	126
P-51 Escort Pilot	128
Bf 109 Pilot	130
Spitfire Pilot	132
Lancaster Crew	134
Ju88 Nightfire	136
U–Boat Captain	138
German Fallschirmjäger	140
US Marine	142
Royal Marine Commando	144
Postwar	**146**
US Special Forces	148
Soviet Spetsnatz	150
French Para	152
Israeli Tank Commander	154
SAS	156
French Foreign Legionary	158

FACTFINDER GUIDE: **WARRIORS**

INTRODUCTION

A WOUNDED UNION SOLDIER ACCEPTS WATER FROM A COMRADE. CIRCA MID-19TH CENTURY

Although violent conflict has been a feature of human life from the earliest times, there is little direct evidence of the nature and techniques, or cause and consequences of prehistoric warfare. Before recorded history, individual human groups probably engaged in sporadic fighting, chiefly raids on rival tribes to gain lands, secure food, or gain valuables. Those involved would have been armed with primitive weapons, mostly constructed from crudely-shaped stone. This type of prehistoric conflict was far from organized, had limited aims, and was probably brief.

The development of what can now be considered warfare, episodes in which trained or semi-trained warriors equipped with weapons designed specifically for fighting, paralleled the creation of regularized, usually settled, societies that had a degree of political leadership and were able to support individuals who were trained and equipped to fight. Such societies had to generate sufficient wealth through trade to support non-productive warriors and provide them with the food and weapons they needed. The earliest evidence for such settled soci-

INTRODUCTION

eties has been uncovered by archeologists at two sites: Jericho at the northern end of the Dead Sea and Catal Huyuk in what is now part of Turkish Anatolia. The cities were walled, suggesting a need for defence and the remains date from 6000 and 7000 BC, respectively.

As the primitive societies developed, they began to invest time and effort in developing the technologies that would allow them the means to wage war successfully. It is clear that metal-working and writing were central to this process. These began in Mesopotamia (modern Iraq), Egypt, China, and the Indus Valley between 3500 and 3000 BC, and the metal was copper. Expensive copper was superseded by bronze, a mixture of copper and tin, around 2500 BC. Bronze, which is easily bent and cannot be honed to a very sharp edge, gave way to stronger and more workable iron in about 1000 BC. It is with the later Bronze Age that the first written records of wars and battles begin and these become more comprehensive from about the sixth century BC. The first battle of which written records remain is Megiddo (1469 BC), which was fought between the Egyptian king Thutmosis III and various rebellious chieftains.

The aims of wars in this period began to resemble those of modern conflict. They began to gain territory or protect land against aggressive neighbors, or seize valuable resources. Initially, wars consisted of a single decisive battle, but as armies expanded, cities were fortified, and other resources were funneled into conflict, they became longer, consisting of more complex maneuvers, several battles, and sieges. The forces involved were also more organized and coordinated. Both the Egyptians and the Assyrians [insert pic 200 not here yet] practiced this type of warfare, although the concept of trained generals and commanders was only slowly developing. Battles of this era generally had little finesse and were decided by brute force.

The soldiers were initially little trained, the mass being drawn from the poorer sections of society. The heart of an army was small, better equipped, and drawn from the upper ranks of society. Close-combat weapons were the ax, mace, dagger, spear, and sword. Firepower was provided by slingers and archers and protection was offered by a shield and armor made from wood, leather, or metal. The best soldiers were at first mounted on chariots, which dominated warfare between around 1700 and 1200 BC. Chariots, which were expensive, were replaced as the key weapon by the individually mounted warrior—cavalry—from about 1000 BC. Previously, horse-breeding was insufficiently developed to produce a mount that could carry the weight of a fully-equipped soldier.

With few exceptions the weapons used by the Ancient Egyptians and others dominated warfare until the employment of gunpowder. However, they did evolve, becoming more robust and effective. The next key changes were the creation of better-trained and-equipped forces, the evolution of new tactics that would make them and their weapons more effective on the battlefield, and the first stirrings of thoughtful generalship. The various types of troops, men armed with close-quarter or missile weapons or mounted soldiers, were organized in separate distinctive units and drawn up for battle in a particular order, usually dense blocks of infantry in the center and cavalry on the flanks. The main tactic was to find a way around an enemy force and attack its vulnerable rear or flanks.

FACTFINDER GUIDE: **WARRIORS**

ALEXANDER THE GREAT AT THE BATTLE OF ISSUS.

However, most leaders found it difficult to control and coordinate their forces once battle was joined, and there was certainly little attempt to improvise tactical maneuvers in the midst of the fighting.

The dominance of the mounted warrior ebbed away between 600 and 400 BC, particularly around the Middle East. The chief impetus for this came from Greece, where mountainous terrain made the employment of cavalry in numbers difficult. Instead, the Greeks focused on creating a powerful infantry arm. These armored and heavily-armed soldiers, known as hoplites, were probably better trained than any infantry seen before and they developed a fighting technique that made the best of their qualities. Known as the phalanx, this was a densely-packed block of hoplites and, although it could not maneuver easily, it proved virtually invulnerable to cavalry and infantry. The flanks of the phalanx were vulnerable, but light infantry equipped with javelins, slings, and bows were used to protect them from attack.

In the hands of Alexander the Great (356-323 BC), [insert pic 201 not here yet] the phalanx won several great victories against the Persian and other empires. However, Alexander's victories relied on him planning battles that made a virtue of the phalanx's strengths and minimized its weaknesses by deploying other forces in its support. Hence, his battles were won by coordinating his various troop types and giving units orders before the fighting began. Alexander was also a master strategist and became an expert at siege warfare. As armies needed bases for resupply and as sanctuaries, the capture of cities became increasingly important and would remain so until well into the age of gunpowder weapons.

Commanders after Alexander continued to develop and improve levels of generalship, notably the Carthaginian general Hannibal Barca (247-183 BC), but it was the Romans who did most to develop the arts of warfare. First, the early Romans instituted a system of compulsory military service, thereby ensuring that Rome had a large pool of trained soldiers who could be employed in times of turmoil. These well-trained, highly motivated soldiers were formed into a tactical formation—the legion—that was highly maneuverable on the battlefield and led by skilled officers. Equipped with throwing javelins, swords, and shields, the individual armored legionary combined the best attributes of both a missile-armed soldier and one equipped for close combat—unlike the phalanx, which it bested in several battles. The Romans also brought

INTRODUCTION

ALEXANDER THE GREAT FACES THE PERSIAN ARMY.

great thought to warfare. Wars were planned in detail and armies were issued with specific objectives while on campaign. They also became masters of siege warfare.

The Roman Empire was eventually overwhelmed, partly due to its own internal weaknesses. Rome itself was sacked in AD 455 and the empire itself is considered to have ended in 476. Although the legion had been the world's best fighting formation for centuries, it had declined in quality from its heyday. Fewer and fewer native Romans joined and ranks were filled with non-Romans, who had less allegiance to the Roman cause. Also, the legion was always weak in cavalry and Roman armies had to rely on foreigners or conquered races to provide this arm. Unfortunately, many of the peoples who assailed the empire in its years of decline were mounted. Clearly they were more mobile that the legion and, although they were less militarily sophisticated than the Romans, these "barbarian" armies effectively combined horsemen who carried missile weapons (especially the bow, which outranged javelins) with those equipped with shock weapons, such as the spear and lance, that could be used in close combat. The defeat of the legion at the hands of mounted warriors signaled the emergence of the mounted warrior as the key type of soldier, a position that would be held for nearly 1,000 years.

The overthrow of Rome heralded an era during which all the ideas on warfare and military thinking developed over the preceding centuries was in great part either ignored or lost to memory. There were, however, exceptions, notably the Byzantine Empire centered on Constantinople (now Istanbul) and the Kingdom of the Franks in Western Europe. The armies of both these states used both infantry and cavalry in battle, but it was their cavalry that was considered to be the elite force.

The Byzantines, essentially the torchbearers for the Roman Empire, were perhaps unique in that they continued to study and analyze warfare as well as military tactics and strategy. They combined this scholarship with an organized military system that was based on trained soldiers fighting in recognizable units under capable generals. Although Byzantine armies probably combined good-quality infantry and cavalry in roughly equal numbers, it was the cavalry that

FACTFINDER GUIDE: **WARRIORS**

RIGHT: A ROMAN SOLDIER CIRCA. 75-100 AD ; FAR RIGHT: HUN CAVALRYMAN

proved to be battle-winners. The best cavalry were known as cataphracts—warriors covered from head to foot in various types of armor and equipped with lances, swords, and bows. In battle, the Byzantines displayed a high degree of coordination between their various forces that was often enormously more sophisticated than those shown by their enemies.

In contrast, Frankish armies combined relatively small numbers of mounted troops supported by a mass of poorer quality foot soldiers. The success of the Franks owed much to their great ruler Charlemagne (724-814). He brought a degree of organization to his forces that had not been seen in Western Europe since the days of the Roman Empire. The Franks were excellent warriors and Charlemagne introduced a system under which his nobles owed him military service in return for the granting of lands. In their turn, the nobles offered protection to lower ranking members of society in return for taxes and military service. This simple system became known as feudalism and came to dominate the organization and conduct of warfare in Western Europe until the end of the close of the 15th century.

Medieval armies, in which the mounted noble and his personal retainers were pre-eminent, were raised only in times of danger and knights were only obliged to serve for a set period. Medieval campaigns were often brief, consisting of just a handful of battles. As medieval societies were based on agriculture, few states could neglect harvest and most lacked the financial resources to support a field army for any length of time. Also, under the feudal system lords had a vested interest in maintaining and protecting the lands they held for their monarch and their own benefit. This was a period of castle building and the capture of such fortifications became a central part of warfare, although more fell to treachery than direct attack.

INTRODUCTION

In open battle, the lordly knights were more concerned with their own personal prestige and were mostly eager to fight an enemy of equal rank. Behind them were masses of poorly trained infantry, often little more than peasants under arms. These were unable to stand up to a thunderous charge delivered by mounted knights for the most part. However, mounted knights could be defeated and it was primarily the English who developed the weapons and tactics to defeat them, heralding the decline of the mounted warrior. The English realized that mounted knights were vulnerable to lightly armed foot soldiers if their charge could be either stopped in its tracks or disorganized. They used longbows to kill or wound knights and their valuable horses before they could use their lances and swords at close range. Knights who reached the English line were often kept at bay with field fortifications such as trenches and lines of stakes. As the wounded, disorganized, and uncoordinated knights milled about these barriers, they would be surrounded by the light infantry, who would use swords, long-bladed knives, and clubs to cut them down. This tactic, repeated frequently during the Hundred Years War (1337-1453), proved remarkably successful.

The second half of the 15th century was marked by the gradual introduction of gunpowder weapons, both cannon and small arms, that heralded the dawn of a new age in warfare. Gunpowder was probably developed in China in the 9th century and the first effective weapons followed in the early 12th century. Although the early weapons were prone to misfiring and were not very accurate at anything more than close range, they did have one great advantage over the longbow. Longbowmen were skilled professionals who had spent years training and perfecting their techniques, whereas training a soldier to fire a gunpowder weapon could be accomplished much more quickly. Gunpowder weapons also brought about the decline of the great stone castles as their walls could be battered down in a few days.

The late 15th and early 16th centuries did not see the complete demise of the armed mounted warrior but did confirm the growing importance of the foot soldier. Early firearms were difficult to load and did not have bayonets. A skilled cavalry commander could, with good timing, launch a charge while the virtually unprotected arquebusiers (early type of musketeer) were reloading. Commanders of infantry needed to prevent the cavalry from charging or getting to grips with the arquebusiers. First the arquebusiers could be protected by trenches and earthworks or in open battle they could shelter under the pikes (long spear) of other infantry. This practice of intermingling of musketeers and pikemen in blocks was to continue in varying degrees until the late 17th century, although the proportion of troops equipped with either pikes or muskets of weapon increasingly favored the latter. This was mainly due to improvements in musket technology and the development of the bayonet, which did away with the need for the protective pikes.

The 17th century saw a revolution in the ways that wars were conducted and fought. As the pike disappeared, commanders needed to maximize the firepower of their musketeers. To this end, they began to organize such units in lines a few ranks deep, allowing the musketeers in the first rank, who could fire no more than two or three rounds a minute, time to fire and reload as the remaining ranks discharged their weapons in sequence. The introduction of the cartridge consisting of a pre-measured charge of gunpowder and musketball also helped to reduce the time taken to reload a musket.

A second major change was the development of standardized units of a strength of between 500 and 1,000 men. These regiments allowed commanders to exercise greater control over their men, engendered great esprit de corps among the troops who served in their ranks, and could be moved about the battlefield with greater speed and precision than ever before. However, as the massed firing of gunpowder weapons quickly covered battlefields in a shroud of dense smoke, commanders often struggled to identify units or discover how the fighting was progressing. Regiments began to dress in brightly colored uniforms so that their officers could separate friend from foe. Cannon also gained a greater degree of mobility in this period. Made in smaller sizes and fitted onto wheeled carriages, they could be moved about the battlefield to support an attack or defeat an enemy advance at close range.

By the end of the 18th century, there was little doubt that, although a massed cavalry charge could have a decisive impact on the outcome of a battle, infantry, particularly if supported by artillery, were increasingly dominant. The scope and extent of warfare in the century was dominated by two factors. First, the economies of societies, especially in Western Europe were still overwhelmingly based on agriculture. Economies could not feed a large field army on campaign for any length of time. Second, the industrial output of the material needed to equip and support a large army was simply not available.

However, this was a century of almost continual warfare in Europe as rival dynasties went to war with their neighbors or embarked on overseas adventures to carve out new colonies. In Europe, armies were not very mobile as they could not forage from the countryside without seriously undermining the rural economy. Consequently, the major powers began to build fortified supply depots often along their borders. Before a campaign could begin, these depots, known as magazines, had to be filled with all the necessary provisions of food and equipment needed to support a large army. These armies were, therefore, handicapped by being tied to the magazines, and the capture or destruction of enemy depots became central to the conduct of wars.

Equally generals had to husband their human resources—their soldiers. Soldiers were costly to maintain and it took time to bring up reinforcements or train replacements. To throw possibly thousands of them away by being defeated in battle was a risk that few commanders were willing to take unless assured of victory. Consequently, many commanders tended to operate within reach of a friendly magazine, which could also function as a fortress into which a defeated army could retreat. However, some commanders, notably the British Duke of Marlborough (1650-1722) during the War of the Spanish Succession (1701-14) and Prussia's Frederick the Great (1712-86) in several mid-18th century wars, demonstrated the strategic vision to move their forces over great distances to put their enemies at a disadvantage.

The armies of the 18th century contained the same types of troops (infantry, cavalry, and artillery), were equipped with very similar weapons and fought in

INTRODUCTION

UNDER ATTACK BY NORTH AMERICAN INDIANS IN THE NORTHWEST TERRITORY CIRCA 1791.

much the same way. Soldiers, who were treated with the greatest severity for even minor infractions of discipline, were not expected to show any initiative but to carry out orders like robots. The aim of the infantry was to close on the enemy as quickly as possible, fire devastating close-range volleys, and then attack with the bayonet. Attacks were supported by artillery fire and cavalry launched charges or pursued retreating enemy forces.

There was little innovation in weaponry or tactics during most of the century. Frederick did develop highly mobile artillery where individual crews were mounted so that they could more easily keep up with infantry or cavalry units. Also a new type of soldier began to appear. This was the light infantryman, who did not fight in the massed ranks of the regular infantry but acted as a skirmisher, taking advantage of cover and firing aimed shots against specific targets, such as officers. Such troop types were found in Europe but were seen more frequently in the American colonies, where the discipline of European-style warfare was less rigorously imposed on the colonial militias.

This highly stylized form of warfare lasted until the latter part of the 18th century. Evidence of change was first evident in the French and Indian Wars in North America (1754-63) and the American War of Independence (1775-83). In North America, difficult terrain (forests, mountains, and few roads) made it impossible for armies to fight in the European manner. Greater flexibility, speed of movement, and a measure of individual initiative became increasingly important.

However, it was France's Revolutionary Wars from 1792 that brought about the most wide-ranging changes in the conduct of warfare. France's pre-

FACTFINDER GUIDE: **WARRIORS**

A PRUSSIAN OFFICER.

Revolutionary army officers had been decimated and, France, which was assailed by several of its neighbors, had to rely on mass conscription of untrained civilians to fight its wars. There was no time to train them in the niceties of 18th century warfare, so they were thrown into battle in dense blocks, which were far easier to handle than long lines of troops. Fired by revolutionary fervor, these troops were able to defeat the invasions that threatened France.

However, the armies of 1800 fought in much the same ways and were equipped with virtually the same range of weapons as those of 1700. However, warfare was transformed by the innovations of one man—Napoleon Bonaparte (1769-1821), emperor of France. Napoleon's genius was to conduct his wars in a totally different way from his contemporaries. The essence of this was speed of maneuver and the rapid concentration of his forces at a point which would most discomfort his enemies. To do this he developed the idea of the all-arms corps. This was a body of troops of all types with a strength of between 20 and 30,000 men. In effect these were miniature armies and big enough to fight alone until reinforced by other corps.

On campaign, Napoleon tried to do away with the need for magazines. His corps, which marched along separate paths, either carried their own food or foraged off the land. They could move at astonishing speeds. If Napoleon was outnumbered by several enemy armies, he would move his forces quickly against one of them, usually defeat it, and then turn on the others one by one. By moving swiftly he tried to fight battles on ground that favored his own plans. Once battle began, Napoleon, who was a superb tactician, used the speed of his troops (who moved in the columns pioneered by the Revolutionary forces) backed by massed cannon fire to crush his opponent. The weakness of Napoleon's tactics were, however, revealed by the British. The Duke of Wellington protected his troops from the worst of the French cannon fire by placing them behind the crests of ridges in the terrain. Thus, they did not sustain the heavy casualties of units that had had to face heavy fire in the open or suffer any drop of morale. As the French attacked in their columns, as at the Battle of Waterloo in 1815, they were met by lines of unshaken infantry firing volleys at close range to which the dense ranks of the column could not reply.

The second half of 19th century saw wide-ranging changes in warfare, primarily because of the impact of industrialization and mass production, which

INTRODUCTION

allowed countries to support and equip vast armies. Railroads allowed commanders to transport troops over long distances in record time and telegraphy gave them the ability to react to sudden events with great speed. Technological developments also had a profound impact on weaponry. The muzzle-loading single-shot musket gave way to first the rifled musket and then the breech-loading rifle, capable of firing several rounds a minute. The accuracy, firepower, and range of weapons improved immeasurably. Artillery, which had undergone similar changes, was now one of the biggest killers in battle.

Because of these great changes in weaponry, it was virtually suicidal to fight in the open at close range. Battles were fought at longer and longer ranges and troops began to fight from prone positions, often from behind field fortifications. The ability to wield a spade became an essential skill. Cavalry were equally unlikely to charge an enemy and, although most leading armies maintained such units and trained them to charge, they were more useful for reconnaissance work and attacks on isolated enemy outposts. They were increasingly likely to fight on foot, using short rifles rather than swords or lances, reserving their mounts for movement at speed. This new type of warfare was perhaps first seen during the American Civil War (1861-65) and later European conflicts, particularly the Franco-Prussian War (1870-71) confirmed the trend.

The impact of more powerful weapons was, in the early years of the 20th century, matched by the development of the internal combustion engine, mechanized transport, and the airplane. Countries had to be able to produce all of these sophisticated but fallible weapons in great quantities. Without them the soldiers in the front line would not be able to fight. This had two consequences. First, every fighting soldier required the efforts of several other individuals to get him into action and keep him fighting. These logistical and support services became important and remain so to the present. Secondly, if it was possible to destroy an enemy's war industries, it would severely weaken his ability to fight on. Thus civilians and war industries many miles away from the fighting became targets. Long-range air power, first airships and later powered bombers could be used to take the war to an enemy's homeland.

All of these factors first coalesced during World War I (1914-18). However, none of the rival commanders fully appreciated the fundamental changes that warfare had undergone within the space of a few decades. For much of the conflict, all believed that a single decisive battle would bring about victory. However, once the war between the Germans against the British and French on the Western Front had been stalemated in trench warfare in late 1914, no side developed the tactics that could win a decisive battle, although both the British and French came close in 1918. The chief problem was that the defenders of a trench held all the advantages. Advancing across the muddy moonscape of no-man's land, the attackers were raked by machine-gun fire, pulverized by massive artillery bombardments, and then became hung up on a thick belt of uncut barbed wire. Even if they captured an enemy position, they were too few in number or too exhausted to exploit any advantage. Reserves earmarked to exploit any success were too slow in arriving because of the problems of crossing no-man's land.

However, World War I did have several important consequences for future wars. First, it highlighted the need to coordinate infantry, artillery, and air power. Second, it showed the need to move both troops and weapons quickly with a degree of protection. Good communications and the further development of mobile weapons using the petrol engine and the creation of large, effective air forces came to dominate the thinking of the more farsighted military theorists. It was in Nazi Germany that the answers to these questions were resolved in the form of Blitzkrieg (lightning war).

Blitzkrieg relied on delivering the maximum amount of firepower (including aircraft) at the quickest possible speed against the weakest part of the enemy's front line. The cutting edge of this strategy was the fast-moving armored division that included not only tanks but also mechanized troops and various types of artillery. Supported by dive-bombers, Nazi Germany's armored divisions overran much of Europe between 1939 and 1941. The basic principles of Blitzkrieg survived the defeat of Nazi Germany in 1945 and the combining of firepower and movement continue to guide military training and war planning down to the present.

Nazi Germany, however, did neglect one aspect of warfare in World War II—amphibious warfare. It was the western Allies, including Britain but above all the United States, that saw the advantageous possibilities of launching infantry attacks from the sea. The invasion of Europe in 1944 and the island-hopping campaigns against the Japanese in the Pacific confirmed that amphibious attacks were practical, if difficult and hazardous. To be effective, it was necessary that such assaults combined specialist troops and equipment, but as the postwar world has confirmed, such capabilities are vital at projecting power across the globe.

Conflict after World War II has been overshadowed by the threat of atomic and then nuclear weapons. Although they have never been used in anger since 1945, soldiers have recently been trained to survive nuclear strikes and continue fighting in their aftermath. However, although such weapons, albeit at huge cost, prevented large-scale wars between the rival superpowers, they have not guaranteed worldwide security or brought about an end to conventional wars.

Since 1945, wars have been of two types. First, those involving the world's leading powers directly. These have occurred because older powers wished to hold onto their colonies in the face of nationalist movements demanding independence or because they have wished to maintain or extend their grip on countries or regions they consider to be within their "spheres of influence." Both types of war often coincide within a particular country and were a particular feature of the Cold War, the struggle for international power between the United States and the Soviet Union. Examples include the Vietnam War (1965-75) and the Soviet occupation of Afghanistan (1979-88). The second type of war or conflict includes fighting between regional rivals in which the leading powers supply weapons and expertise to one side or the other in the hope of maintaining influence within the client state but do not involve their own forces in the fighting.

INTRODUCTION

BRITISH GAS SENTRY, WORLD WAR I.

Such wars have often pitted large, well-equipped and technologically sophisticated armies against those with few military skills, who have resorted to guerrilla warfare to achieve their aims. The guerrillas do not rely on sophisticated technology and typically avoid pitched battles in which they cannot hope to match the resources of their opponents. Rather, they rely on ambushes and hit-and-run raids to demoralize and weaken an enemy's resolve. Only when the guerrillas have built up their military resources and judge the enemy sufficiently weakened do they engage in more conventional types of warfare. Guerrilla movements have been remarkably successful in many parts of the world since 1945.

The history of warfare from prehistory to the present day has many strands. Without doubt technology has always played a key role in the outcome of a war. Those who can afford increasingly sophisticated weapons in sufficient numbers have a marked advantage over less well-equipped foes. However, any study of warfare also shows that technology is not sufficient in itself to ensure victory. The technology has to be given to soldiers who have the training to get the best out of the it. A modern attack helicopter or a missile system, for example, are useless if no one understands how to use them. Equally, there needs to be someone in charge who understands the bigger picture and who knows how to deploy the technology to its maximum effect. Thus command, from the lowliest officer to a senior general, is a vital component of warfare.

Nevertheless, warfare is much more than technology and generalship. At its most basic, it is to do with the individual soldier, for it is him (and occasionally her) who has to face an enemy and carry out an officer's orders, and thus be prepared to die. Soldiers have joined an army and gone to war for many reasons. Poverty, the possibility of wealth, glory, comradeship, compulsion, and the belief in the justice of a cause have all motivated civilians to join up. As the following examples of warriors through the ages show, no single factor decides why one soldier is better than another. However a combination of factors, such as training and equipment, well-being, the provision of medical services, regular pay, or comradeship for example, can make one warrior significantly more effective than another.

17

FACTFINDER GUIDE: **WARRIORS**

Sumerian Infantry

THIRD MILLENNIUM BC

A CARVING OF SUMERIAN SOLDIERS ON A ROYAL TOMB.

The Sumerians, who inhabited a number of warring city-states in Mesopotamia, the area between the Tigris and Euphrates River in what is now Iraq, provide historians with the first written records of warfare. Evidence for their wars and the nature of their arms come from two main sources—the "Standard of Ur" (a mosaic) and a memorial to a war, known as the "Stele of the Vultures," (a stele is a type of obelisk) between the rival cities of Lagash and Umma.

The Ur Standard shows a Sumerian army consisting of spear-armed infantry supported by four-wheeled chariots. The bulk of the army comprised bare-foot infantry equipped with thrusting spears. They are shown wearing long cloaks worn over tunics and are barefooted; their heads are protected by close-fitting caps. They are attacking in a close formation with their spears leveled, presenting a hedge of points to the enemy. It seems likely that the chariots provided the elite of the early Sumerian army, while the infantry made up the slower-moving bulk around which the charioteers operated.

SUMERIAN INFANTRY

The later Stele of the Vultures clearly shows that Sumerian armies were innovators. In particular, the infantry are significantly different from those depicted in the earlier Ur Standard. The infantry have given up the cloak but kept the close-fitting helmet. However, most significantly, they are carrying large shields reaching from the level of the neck to the ankle. These are dotted with disks, probably of bronze. It has been suggested that these could be used to reflect sunlight into an enemy's eyes. The infantry on the stele are equipped with longer spears that those depicted on the Ur Standard, and they have formed up in a densely-packed mass with their spears leveled at chest height.

Although the stele is incomplete, and the missing fragments may have shown other troop types, it seems clear that these heavy infantry had an important role in later Sumerian warfare. Their formation suggests a precursor to the Greek phalanx of hoplites. The Sumerian spear phalanx was a fairly basic formation and its tactics may have consisted of advancing on the enemy as quickly as possible, probably after the supporting chariots had weakened the enemy by throwing spears. The flanks of the block of the spearmen might have been protected with lighter infantry, men armed with spears but without shields. However, as with the phalanx, the Sumerian spearmen were vulnerable on broken terrain, which probably made it difficult for them to keep their cohesion. Equally, the close-packed ranks might have been vulnerable to more lightly equipped infantry who could have darted in between the spears to strike blows against the Sumerians.

Sumerian warfare was not sophisticated and military leadership was basic. Commanders were supposed to lead by example, fighting hand to hand against a worthy opponent to win glory. Nevertheless, the evidence from Sumeria, although fragmentary, does indicate that military technology was evolving, and that the armies of the time had at least rudimentary tactics on the battlefield.

ALEXANDER THE GREAT FACES THE PERISAN ARMY.

FACT BOX

| NATIONALITY | **SUMERIAN** |
| LOCATION | **MESOPOTAMIA** |

CAMPAIGNS
Various wars between rival cities

TYPE: **INFANTRY**

FACTFINDER GUIDE: **WARRIORS**

Egyptian Charioteer

c. 1294 BC

A CHARIOT AND ITS ATTENDANT.

The Egyptians learned the military value of chariots, of which they had no previous experience, from the Hyksos, who invaded Egypt in c. 1800 BC and had subjugated much of the country by c. 1700 BC. The Hyksos were eventually defeated by Amosis, who drove them from Egypt between 1580 and 1157 BC. Amosis completely rebuilt Egypt's armies, creating the country's first standing army. Chariots were a key part of the new army and they dominated warfare in the ancient Middle East until around 1200 BC.

Egyptian chariots, made of wood, were notably different from other types. The gave the appearance of being flimsy and were certainly lightweight. This may have been for two reasons. First, the horses of the day were not the thoroughbreds of today and were not up to pulling or carrying heavy loads. Indeed, the Egyptians had no cavalry units. Second, because of the soft sand and rocky terrain that covered much of the kingdom, it may have been thought that lighter chariots had a better chance of avoiding becoming bogged down or being damaged by collisions.

Egyptian chariots were pulled by two smallish horses and also tended to have fewer crewmen than their rivals, usually just a driver and a single archer, whose quiver was attached to the side of the chariot. The archer wore armor consisting of a leather tunic that was sometimes covered with scale armor. The leather was usually sufficient to protect the wearer against glancing sword cuts or spear thrusts. His weapon was a composite bow made from several materials that had an effective range of around 220 yards.

Egyptian chariots were an attempt to combine battlefield mobility with firepower, and were not primarily designed to slug it out with an enemy in hand to hand combat. Rather their role was to close on the enemy and then use the archers to kill or wound as many as possible. Charioteers were trained to charge at an enemy, allow their archers to fire, and then turn about. The tactic being repeated as necessary.

Egyptian chariots did much to drive the Hyksos invaders from Egypt and then expand the frontiers of the kingdom. At Megiddo in 1479 BC (the first recorded battle in history), the Egyptians, led by Thutmosis III, won a great victory over various rebel tribes in Palestine. Victory was assured by a devastating chariot charge, which shattered the rebel forces and sent them fleeing from the field of battle.

Perhaps the greatest chariot battle of the Egyptian era was fought at Kadesh in 1294 BC, when Egyptian and Hittite forces, including a total of over 6,000 chariots, clashed. The battle was technically a draw, but also showed the potential weakness of Egyptian chariots. They were not really designed to fight at close quarters, but at Kadesh had to charge the heavier, stronger Hittite chariots. The Hittite chariots also carried infantry armed with spears and iron weapons, which were much more effective in close combat that the bronze weapons used by the Egyptians. Kadesh was the highpoint of chariot warfare, but chariots began to disappear thereafter. Horses were being bred that could carry the weight of a fully-equipped warrior. Expensive and fragile chariots had had their day, the mounted soldier was the way forward.

FACT BOX

NATIONALITY **ANCIENT EGYPTIAN**
LOCATION **NILE DELTA AND PALESTINE**

CAMPAIGNS
Served in various Egyptian wars between c. 1580-c. 1200 BC

TYPE: **INFANTRY**

FACTFINDER GUIDE: **WARRIORS**

Assyrian Archer

EIGHTH CENTURY BC

AN ASSYRIAN ARCHER WITH HIS SHIELD BEARER.

The Assyrians, whose homeland was in what is now northern Iraq, created one of the greatest empires of the ancient world. From about the middle of the 14th century BC, they embarked on wars of conquest which would establish a regime that controlled a huge swathe of territory stretching from the Persian Gulf to the coast of the eastern Mediterranean and down through Palestine into northern Egypt. The extraordinary successes of the Assyrians owed much to the fact that they were great military innovators. The empire reached its zenith under the later Assyrian kings, particularly Tiglath-Pileser III who ruled between 745 and 727 BC.

One of the Assyrians' great innovations was to revitalize the role of their infantry by equipping many of them with the composite bow, which enabled them to strike at targets at long range. Although Assyrian cavalry and chariot units were used to weaken and disorganize an enemy force, it was the infantry that delivered the most telling blow. Archers appear to have been divided into heavy, medium, and light types. Heavy archers

22

ASSYRIAN ARCHER

wore long tunics of scale armor and their heads were protected by helmets. It also appears that, in sieges at least, the heavy archers were accompanied by a shield-carrier. The shield was made of wicker, the height of a man, and curved at the top. This was designed to protect the archer from arrows fired down from the ramparts of an enemy city while he sought a target or reloaded. Medium archers wore less armor and may have also been protected by a shield-bearer. The light archers did not wear armor or helmet, relying instead on their agility to protect them from an enemy. Some of the archers at least were equipped with a sword for close combat.

In open battle, the Assyrians gradually evolved tactics that made the best of the various troop types available to them. Their charioteers and horse-mounted troops, many of who also carried bows, were deployed to prevent an enemy from getting close to the Assyrian infantry but keep them at a range where the massed fire from the foot archers could be most effective.

Spear-armed infantry would then attack and if the enemy were routed they would be pursued by cavalry. The Assyrians were, thus, one of the first civilizations to combine the various types of soldiers available to them into an effective and cooperative whole.

The Assyrians were also masters of siege warfare. Enemies defeated in the field would often retreat into fortresses they considered to be impregnable. However, the Assyrians developed sophisticated techniques to deal with strong walls and towers. Once an assault had been decided upon, the archers had a key role to play. Their job was to unleash volleys of arrows against the enemy ramparts, thereby allowing the attacking infantry the opportunity to scale the walls without suffering severe casualties. The Assyrians became masters of the art of siege warfare. The empire, however, did not survive and it eventually fell prey to internal divisions. In 612 BC, the Assyrian capital Nineveh, was captured and destroyed after a three-year siege.

FACT BOX

NATIONALITY **ASSYRIAN**
LOCATION **MIDDLE EAST, EGYPT**

CAMPAIGNS
Various wars of conquest

TYPE: **ARCHER**

FACTFINDER GUIDE: **WARRIORS**

Persian Immortal

5TH CENTURY BC

THE PERSIAN HORSEMAN DEPICTED WAS PROBABLY A LEADER'S BODYGUARD.

By the early 5th century BC, the Persian Empire covered much of what is now the Middle East and beyond to the gates of the Indian sub-continent. The military power of the empire was enormous and successive emperors had attempted to use their armies to invade and conquer the various city-states that made up Ancient Greece. In 480 BC the Persian emperor of the time, Xerxes, ordered a bridge of boats to be built across the Hellespont, the stretch of water separating Asia Minor from Europe, and led an army estimated at 150,000 men against Greece. One of his finest units was the 10,000-strong corps of Immortals, so named that no matter what its battle losses it was always brought back up to full strength as quickly as possible.

The Immortals were all Persians; members of races conquered by the Persians were ineligible to join their ranks. Successive Persian emperors lavished fortunes on the Immortals. Their ceremonial uniforms consisted of extravagant, flowing tunics, although their clothes were less ornate

24

PERSIAN IMMORTAL

on campaign. A corselet of scale armor was sometimes worn under the robe. The highly trained and disciplined Immortals were a type of dual-purpose infantry as is confirmed by the weapons each carried.

These consisted of bows and seven-foot spears. The aim was to combine firepower (the bow) with a shock weapon (the spear). However, it also seems likely that some Immortals were equipped with a shield and spear, and it is unlikely that these troops would have carried a bow as well. The difficulty of handling three pieces of equipment at the same time probably meant that the Immortals in the front ranks may have carried just the spear and shield, while those behind were equipped with just the bow and spear. The basic tactic was for the front ranks to advance on an enemy, while the bowmen advancing behind them weakened their opponents with their arrows.

The Immortals were an impressive sight, but as troops they had several weaknesses that would undermine their effectiveness against more resolute opponents. Two of their glaring shortcomings were that they did not wear helmets and did not carry swords. They were also lightly armored. If the Immortals carrying protective shields could be defeated then the archers had little or no protection. These basic limitations were made plain during the Persian Empire's wars against Greece. The Greek city-states had the ideal soldier to combat the Immortals—the hoplite. These heavily armored infantrymen also carried shields and wielded spears that were longer than those carried by the Immortals. They were also equipped with swords and were probably even better trained that the Immortals.

The Persian invasion of 480 BC was decisively defeated. Xerxes' army won a victory over a much smaller force of Greek hoplites at Thermopylae, but his casualties were enormous and the Greeks were only defeated after being attacked from all sides. However, the disaster at Thermopylae was avenged at the naval Battle of Salamis. This overwhelming Greek victory forced Xerxes and the bulk of his army to withdraw back across the Hellespont.

A PERSIAN IMMORTAL EQUIPPED WITH BOW, SHIELD AND SPEAR.

FACT BOX

NATIONALITY **PERSIAN**
LOCATION **MIDDLE EAST**

CAMPAIGNS
Various Greek and Persian wars

TYPE: **MEDIUM INFANTRY**

25

FACTFINDER GUIDE: **WARRIORS**

Spartan Hoplite

5TH CENTURY BC

A SPARTAN HOPLITE IN FULL MILITARY GEAR.

Sparta was one of several city-states that made up ancient Greece, and is widely regarded as the home of the finest soldiers of the period—the hoplites. Because much of Greece is mountainous, the ancient Greeks had few cavalry, preferring to rely on foot soldiers, who made up the overwhelming bulk of their armies. Sparta was a militaristic society in which all suitable males trained from an early age (seven) as warriors. Becoming a hoplite was a great honor; so much so that all had to provide their own weapons and equipment.

The Spartan hoplites trained together for years and shared the same barracks as well. Consequently, their *esprit de corps*, morale, and fighting abilities were unrivaled during the period. Indeed, all Spartan hoplites were trained to believe that it was better to die on the battlefield that live to tell of any defeat.

The hoplite's equipment was fairly standardized. It consisted of a large round shield (hoplon, hence the name hoplite) around three feet in diameter. Many Spartan shields carried the Greek letter "lamba" (an inverted "v")

26

SPARTAN HOPLITE

which stood for "Lakedaemon," the correct name for Sparta. Armor consisted of a plumed helmet that covered the crown of the head and neck. The cheeks and nose were protected by flanges. The upper body was protected by a leather waistcoat, which was laced at the front and covered with iron scales. Similar flaps covered the shoulders and greaves protected the lower leg. These were initially of bronze but this gave way to lighter and more flexible leather. A hoplite's weapons consisted of a spear up to nine feet long and a sword.

The tactics of the hoplites were fairly simple. Moving into the attack, they would form dense, tight-packed blocks, known as phalanxes, usually between eight and 16 men deep. This then moved against an enemy as quickly as possible. Its speed and the hoplites discipline and fighting skills, usually ensured that the phalanx was difficult to defeat. The hoplites would crash into the enemy's front line, using their spears to stab opponents and their shields to knock them off balance, and then resort to their swords.

The Spartan phalanx of hoplites could be beaten, however. Both the phalanx as a whole and the hoplites had certain weaknesses. First, the phalanx was most effective on flat, open terrain. Rugged, broken ground could often disorganize a phalanx, making the hoplite more vulnerable, particularly to cavalry attack. Secondly, the hoplites had to carry a lot of weight and it was easy for them to tire in prolonged combat. Thirdly, they did not have any missile weapons, particularly slings and bows. If the enemy's archers, javelinmen, and slingers could avoid close combat with the hoplites, they could use their missiles to cause casualties to the phalanx without it being able to reply. Many Greek armies began to employ their own light infantry of this type, known as "peltasts," to keep the opposing archers and the like out of range of the hoplites. Nevertheless, as several great victories, such as Marathon in 490, against the Persians confirmed, the phalanx was a powerful battlefield weapon.

FACT BOX

| NATIONALITY | **SPARTAN** |
| LOCATION | **ANCIENT GREECE** |

CAMPAIGNS
Greek civil wars, Greek- Persian wars

TYPE: **HEAVY INFANTRY**

FACTFINDER GUIDE: **WARRIORS**

Carthaginian Cavalry

LATE 2ND CENTURY BC

CARTHAGINIAN CAVALRYMEN OR "HANIBAL'S ARMY" WERE AN ECLECTIC MIX OF NATIONS.

Carthage, a city-state based in what is now Tunisia, founded in the ninth century BC, carved out a great maritime empire along the shores of the Mediterranean and by the third century BC had come into conflict with the Romans. A series of conflicts followed, known as the Punic Wars after the Roman term for the founders of Carthage. There were three Punic Wars, the first beginning in 265 BC, and Rome eventually destroyed Carthage in 146 BC at the climax of the third. However, the Carthaginians came close to destroying the Roman world during the second war fought between 219 and 202 BC. Under the inspired leadership of Hannibal Barca (247-183 BC), the Carthaginians invaded Roman Italy from the north in 218 BC and inflicted a series of catastrophic defeats on the Romans, not least at the Battle of Lake Trasimene (217 BC), where his forces killed 30,000 Roman troops.

Hannibal's victories were all the more remarkable because his forces were drawn from the many peoples who had been conquered by Carthage. Among the finest of these

28

CARTHAGINIAN CAVALRY

came from Numidia (modern Algeria). The Numidians (the name is derived from the Latin for "land of the nomads") provided the Carthaginian army with light horsemen. They were skilled riders, who controlled their horses by voice or a stick as they used neither the bit nor the bridle and rode bareback. Their small horses were, however, hardy, fleet of foot, and agile. The Numidians wore their everyday dress—a sleeveless tunic. The only protection they carried into battle was a small shield. The weapons used by the Numidian cavalry included throwing javelins and spears. Although the evidence is contradictory, they do not seem to have generally carried either swords or knives.

The Numidians were not used to take on heavier enemy cavalry, although as the Romans lacked a strong cavalry arm, this was not a problem in the Punic Wars. Their chief role was to use their speed and agility to harass an enemy with their javelins and then fall back before their opponents could respond. Numidians rarely made charges against a well-formed enemy, preferring to attack from ambushes, launch hit-and-run raids, or pursue a demoralized foe. In these roles they excelled.

At Cannae in 216BC, they played a key role in Hannibal's greatest victory. When the battle was over, 60,000 Romans lay dead on the field of battle. At the outset, the Numidian light cavalry were engaged in an inconclusive combat with elements of the Roman cavalry, who were eventually driven from the field after the arrival of other Carthaginian cavalry. The Numidians took over the pursuit of their defeated opponents, while the rest of the Roman army was annihilated.

The Romans learned great lessons from the defeat at Cannae. In 202 they inflicted a decisive defeat on Hannibal at Zama, which effectively ended the second Punic War. The Roman commander, Scipio Africanus, had been able to persuade one Numidian ruler to desert the Carthaginian cause and provide troops for Rome. Among these were 4,000 of the light cavalry that had previous contributed to Hannibal's previous victories.

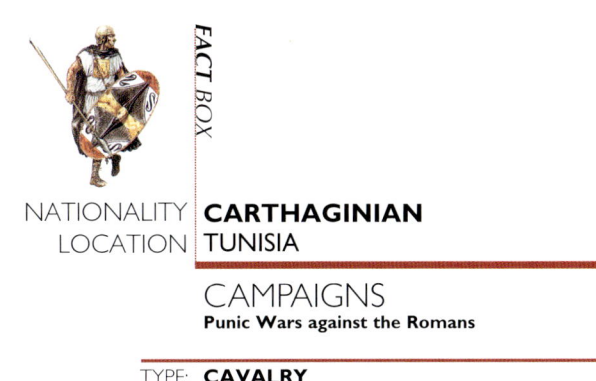

FACT BOX

NATIONALITY **CARTHAGINIAN**
LOCATION **TUNISIA**

CAMPAIGNS
Punic Wars against the Romans

TYPE: **CAVALRY**

FACTFINDER GUIDE: **WARRIORS**

Roman Legionnaire

FIRST CENTURY BC

ROMAN SOLDIERS OF THIS ERA WERE TRAINED, EQUIPPED AND CARED FOR BY THE STATE.

Shortly before the beginning of the first century BC, the armies of the Roman republic were transformed by the actions of one man, Gaius Marius (157-86BC). Marius, although the son of a peasant, had risen through the ranks of the republican army and had been elected consul. From this position of power, he began root-and-branch reforms that would make Roman armies virtually unbeatable for centuries.

Among Marius's most important reforms was that soldiers no longer had to buy their own weapons and equipment. Henceforth they were provided by the state. Thus even poor Roman citizens could join the armed forces. They then had to serve for 16 years. Although the legion commander was appointed by the general, junior officers gained their rank on length of service or merit. However, Marius's major efforts were directed to restructuring the legion. He swept away the various old troop types and equipped legionnaires with the same standardized equipment—a short thrusting sword ("gladius") and light and heavy javelins ("pila"). The javelins had a long, thin shaft of iron, which made them bend when striking a target. This meant that they could not be thrown back at the

30

ROMAN LEGIONNAIRE

legionnaire. Equally, the pilum was heavy enough to penetrate deep into an enemy shield, making it difficult to extract. Legionnaires were also given standardized armor—a large, usually rectangular, shield as well as body armor to protect the upper body and head.

Marius also transformed the organization of the legion, making it a flexible formation capable of rapid movement. A Marian legion comprised ten cohorts of between 400 and 500 legionnaires. Each cohort would form up in battle eight or ten men deep with a frontage of 50 men. In battle, the cohorts were arranged in three lines, with four cohorts in the front line and three each in the second and third lines. The individual cohorts were widely spaced. When advancing or throwing their javelins, the individual legionnaires in close order occupied a frontage of three feet, but required six feet when they were engaged in hand to hand fighting. Consequently each cohort had to extend its frontage by 100 percent when changing from close to more open order. Hence the cohort-wide gaps between individual cohorts.

Roman battle tactics were straightforward. Shower the enemy with javelins at fairly close range and then charge to close quarters where the short swords would be used against the shaken enemy line. However, the chief advantages that the legion had over its foes were the discipline and training of its legionnaires.

Marius also developed the engineering skills of the legion. Individual legionnaires were expected to be able to march 20 miles a day carrying large amounts of equipment, including the tools needed to build the forts that protected the legion each night while on campaign. The legionnaires became masters of construction, whether forts, bridges, roads, or the extensive border fortifications (limes), such as Hadrian's Wall in northern England, which were designed to protect Rome's distant frontiers. Marius's reforms created the legion structure on which the Roman Empire was built.

ONE OF MARIUS'S "MULES."

FACT BOX

NATIONALITY	**ROMAN**
LOCATION	**ROMAN REPUBLIC AND EMPIRE**

CAMPAIGNS
Rome's numerous wars

TYPE: **INFANTRY**

31

FACTFINDER GUIDE: **WARRIORS**

Byzantine Cavalry

6TH CENTURY

After the fall of the Rome in the fifth century AD, the remnants of the once-great power were based in the city of Byzantium, later Constantinople. Although the Byzantine Empire was assailed on all sides and lost considerable territory, during the reign of Emperor Justinian (483-565) the empire regained many of its former lands. Justinian was fortunate in two of his generals—Belisarius (c. 505-565) and Narses (478-573). Both men commanded armies that were usually much smaller than those of the empire's enemies. In particular, Belisarius reconquered North Africa from the Vandals, winning great victories at Ad Decimum and Tricameron in 533, when his army was outnumbered by four or five-to-one. He later captured Rome (536) from the Goths and then managed to hold the city for two years while besieged by around 50,000 Goths. Byzantine armies contained infantry, but their great strength lay with their heavily armored cavalry, known as "cataphracts."

Cataphracts were encased in various types of armor from head to foot. Typically this would include a chain-mail shirt stretching from neck to thigh. The feet were covered in

BYZANTINE CAVALRY

metal shoes, while the lower legs were protected by greaves. Hands were protected by gauntlets, and the head by a conical helmet. Small shields were fixed to the left arm, leaving the cataphract's hands free to control his horse, which was also covered in armor, and wield his weapons. A cataphract's weapons included a large sword, 12 foot lance, dagger, and bow.

Cataphracts were highly trained in the use of their weapons, but were also taught a series of battlefield drills that made them the best, most disciplined cavalry of their age. The great strength of the cataphracts owed much to the way they were deployed and used by generals such as Belisarius and Narses. Byzantine infantry invariably formed up in the center, with units of light cavalry and cataphracts on the flanks and at the rear. The spear-armed infantry, often protected by ditches or stakes, usually absorbed the first enemy attacks. If these were stopped and the enemy disorganized, light cavalry armed with bows were used to inflict further casualties at range and then the cataphracts would be unleashed.

Charging against unformed infantry or lighter cavalry, the cataphracts were devastating. Virtually invulnerable because of their armor, their charges, delivered in close-packed ranks could sweep all before them. The favored mode of attack involved charges against an enemy unit's flanks or rear. A cavalry reserve would then be thrown against the shaken enemy.

The great victories won by Belisarius were achieved by this combination of defensive and offensive tactics. He realized that his enemies were less disciplined that his own forces. His tactic in open battle was to "encourage" the enemy to attack. He might, for example, place his infantry in a seemingly vulnerable position, keeping his powerful cavalry arm in reserve. Belisarius, thanks to his heavy cavalry, won many victories for Justinian, but fell foul of palace politics. He was imprisoned in 562 on suspicions of treachery, but was released 12 months later.

BYZANTINE WARRIORS WERE KNOWN FOR BEING COVERED IN ARMOR FROM HEAD TO TOE.

FACT BOX

| NATIONALITY | **BYZANTINE** |
| LOCATION | **BYZANTINE EMPIRE** |

CAMPAIGNS
Wars of Justinian

TYPE: **HEAVY CAVALRY**

33

FACTFINDER GUIDE: **WARRIORS**

Arthurian Cavalryman

SIXTH CENTURY

FEW IMAGES SURVIVE FROM THIS PERIOD; THIS PICTISH HORSEMAN IS FROM THE LATE DARK AGES.

By the late fifth century, the Roman presence in Britain had all but disappeared. What military forces remained consisted of the few remaining Roman troops and the so-called "Combrogi" (meaning "fellow-countrymen"), who were Romanized Britons. The once united country slowly split into a number of regional kingdoms ruled by Duces, who often set up their headquarters in hill-top earthworks. Gradually the Romano-British, Christian kingdoms succumbed to external invasion and, by the early sixth century, were particularly under increased threat from Saxon invaders.

Although evidence is scanty, it is thought that one Romano-British chieftain, Arthur, held a measure of supreme authority over the other Duces and strove to defeat the pagan Saxons by uniting the kingdoms against them. Accordingly, he was granted the title "Dux Bellorum," meaning "Leader of Battles." Arthur's wars began well, with a decisive victory at the unidentified Mount Baden, but ended some 20 years later with defeat at Camlan, where he was killed.

ARTHURIAN CAVALRYMAN

His loss signaled the end of Romano-British resistance to the Saxons.

Arthur's Romano-British forces consisted of both infantry and cavalry. Although the infantry, who fought in dense lines or individual groups, formed the bulk of the Arthurian forces, it was the cavalry who often had a decisive impact in the campaigns against the Saxons, particularly as the Saxons fought exclusively on foot. The cavalry, the vast majority of whom were drawn from the Romano-British nobility, were used to launch ambushes and raids on Saxon settlements, but in formal battle they operated on the flanks of the foot soldiers. However, it was the frequent hit-and-run raids and ambushes that did much to weaken the Saxon efforts to subjugate the Romano-British.

Arthur's cavalry were equipped with spears with ash shafts, javelins to fling at an enemy at close and medium ranges, swords, and daggers. Most would carry two or three foot oval, or occasionally circular, shields of a modified Roman design made of alder faced with hide. Clothing would also reflect the influence of Roman fashions and trends—the better equipped cavalry wore chain mail corselets, which covered the upper body and reached to the knees, and helmets, which in the case of prominent leaders or officers might be fitted with a plume. Long, flowing woollen cloaks were also popular

In formal battles, the cavalry might launch charges against the enemy or advance to a range from where they could throw their javelins to break up the Saxon line. Records also suggest that Arthurian cavalry often tried to tempt the Saxons into a wild, uncoordinated charge by faking sudden retreats. But they would also be used to pursue a retreating enemy.

Arthur's death and the success of the Saxon wars of conquest effectively ended the role of cavalry in British warfare for several hundred years. The Saxons were primarily foot soldiers and it was not until their catastrophic defeat at the hands of Norman cavalry at the Battle of Hastings in 1066 that mounted warriors again had a significant role in local wars.

FACT BOX

| NATIONALITY | **ROMANO-BRITISH** |
| LOCATION | **BRITAIN** |

CAMPAIGNS
Saxon invasions

TYPE: **MEDIUM/LIGHT CAVALRY**

FACTFINDER GUIDE: **WARRIORS**

Arab Cavalryman

9TH CENTURY

ARAB CAVALRYMEN WERE AMONG THE MOST FEARED WARRIORS OF THEIR TIME.

When the Prophet Mohammed, the founder of the Islamic religion, died in 632 his teachings had united the various peoples of Arabia. Over the following centuries, they and their descendants carved out a great empire that stretched from Asia Minor to Persia, and across North Africa into Spain. His followers were fired by religious fervor, believing that all who fell in a jihad (holy war) would automatically enter heaven. This Islamic Empire eventually succumbed to factional infighting and effectively ended by the beginning of the 11th century. However, for nearly 400 years the Arabs were among the most feared soldiers in the world.

Although Arab armies did include infantry, their cutting edge in the later

36

ARAB CAVALRYMAN

centuries was formed by cavalry units. Apart from light cavalry, Arab forces also contained a number of heavier units. Cavalrymen in these formations held a higher status and tended to wear long chainmail coats known as a "zardfaa" that reached to the knees and mail caps that covered the crown of the head and neck. Tall helmets also protected their heads and the lower legs might be protected by wood or metal greaves. Less wealthy heavy cavalrymen would make do with leather or quilted felt armor; both types being effective at deflecting glancing sword cuts.

The equipment carried by the cavalry consisted of a circular shield, a lance ("rumh") often with a bamboo shaft, a sword, and possibly a mace. The straight sword, known as a "saif," was made out of iron and later steel, while the mace, often carried between the knee and stirrup staff, was of metal and could be either thrown or wielded in close combat. There is some evidence to suggest that the ax was also carried by some cavalry.

Arab cavalry fought in large blocks, possibly on the decimal system, the smallest being the "khamsah" of just five men. The largest being possibly 10,000. On the eve of battle, cavalry units would form in a block five deep and then charge en masse, often preceded by light cavalry who acted as skirmishers. However, Arab cavalry was also renowned for the ability to stage a fake retreat in the hope of drawing an enemy away from a strong position. They would then turn about and renew their attack on more favorable terms. Ambushes were another tactic popular with Arab armies. In such attacks the cavalry tended to attack in smaller groups, probing for weakness in an enemy's formation.

These armies proved formidable opponents. At the Battle of Qadisiyya against the Persians in 637, they were outnumbered by two-to-one, but the three-day battle ended in victory. However, their attempts to advance into Northern Europe from Spain ended with defeat at the Battle of Tours in 732. Here, they faced resolute Frankish infantry who were able to beat off repeated attacks by the Arab cavalry. The Arabs withdrew back into Spain and effectively gave up any hope of conquering lands in what is now France.

FACT BOX

NATIONALITY	**VARIOUS MUSLIM PEOPLES**
LOCATION	**MIDDLE EAST, NORTH AFRICA, SPAIN**

CAMPAIGNS
Various wars of expansion

TYPE: **HEAVY CAVALRY**

FACTFINDER GUIDE: **WARRIORS**

Frankish Cavalryman

9TH CENTURY

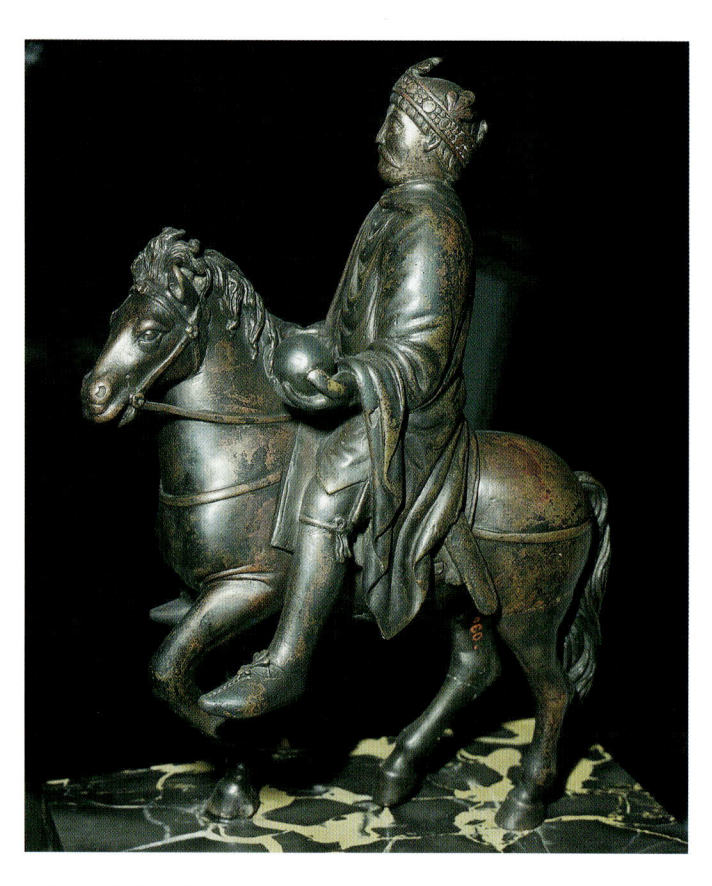

BRONZE EQUESTRIAN STATUE OF CHARLEMAGNE.

The Franks founded a dynasty based in what is now France, and gradually came to rule much of Western Europe. Their empire emerged in the mid-eighth century and survived until the latter decades of the tenth century. One of their major legacies to medieval Europe was the social order of feudalism, in which nobles received lands from the ruler in exchange for tribute and provision of soldiers in times of danger. The cutting edge of any Frankish force in the latter years of the empire was its heavy cavalry.

Frankish heavy cavalry wore armor. Chiefly a one-piece chain mail corselet, which protected the upper body, arms, and legs. Each lower leg would be protected by flexible metal, or occasionally leather, greaves, while one arm—the right—was also protected by an armored vambrace from wrist to upper arm. The left arm, which carried a circular shield was left unarmored. A leather or quilted jacket was sometimes worn under the corselet and had two functions. First, it cushioned the body against heavy blows;

these might not cut through the chain mail but could cause severe bruising. Second, the jacket prevented the chain mail links piercing the skin.

Heavy cavalry carried a variety of weapons into battle. The spear was usually thrust overarm or thrown at an enemy, although there is evidence that the Franks were also using the weapon as a lance. This spear/lance had a "winged" head that was designed to prevent the spearhead from penetrating too far into an enemy's body (as this would make it difficult to extract). Swords (the Franks were widely held to be the best swordmakers in Europe at the time) were long and broad-bladed and used for cutting rather than thrusting at a target. Some warriors may have also carried a knife—the broad-bladed "scramaseax." Records also suggest that heavy cavalrymen had to provide themselves with bows and arrows, but there is little evidence that they were used on horseback. Frankish cavalry of this period had developed stirrups on their saddles, a revolutionary innovation that gave them better balance and superior control over their mounts.

Frankish armies contained both infantry and cavalry, and both types formed up in dense, close-packed bodies prior to going into action. The major tactic of the cavalry was the charge, although their is evidence that they were equally at home fighting on foot. A contemporary chronicle also records that Frankish cavalry were willing to dismount if surrounded, form a shield wall, and fight back-to-back. During the initial charge, cavalry relied on their spears but, once close-quarter battle was joined they made use of their swords.

The Franks had to defend their frontiers from many raiders, including the Vikings of Scandinavia. Cavalry, often operating from border fortifications, would move quickly to block an incursion or launch counter-raids. Under pressure on all sides, the Franks even granted land in their kingdom to certain bands of Vikings in return for protecting the empire from other Viking raiders. In 911, the Frankish ruler Charles the Simple gave Normandy in northern France to one band of Vikings. These people settled and intermarried, becoming known as Normans.

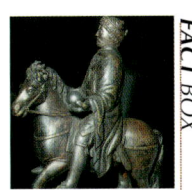

FACT BOX

NATIONALITY **FRANKS**
LOCATION **WESTERN EUROPE**

CAMPAIGNS
Border raids and incursions

TYPE: **HEAVY CAVALRYMAN**

FACTFINDER GUIDE: **WARRIORS**

Viking Hersir

11TH CENTURY

"BERSERKS BITING THEIR SHIELDS" — NORSE CHESSMEN FROM THE ISLE OF LEWIS, SCOTLAND.

The Vikings of Scandinavia were the greatest seafarers—and most feared raiders—of their age. From the late eight to the mid-11th century, their longboats, each carrying 30 or 40 men, spread terror along the coasts of Europe. Raiding parties could vary between a few hundred and several thousand men. They even penetrated deep along the rivers of what is now Russia and may have reached North America. Although primarily raiders, some Vikings settled in the lands they assaulted or became mercenaries for local rulers. A key part of the Viking military structure was the "hersir," a local military commander. Owing loyalty to a local lord ("jarl"), hersirs was responsible for maintaining around 20 or so warriors each.

A typical hersir would wear a short chain mail shirt to protect his upper body and a usually conical helmet with or without a band to protect the nose. Horned hemets owe more to Hollywood movies than historical accuracy! His shield was between two and three feet in width and constructed from a variety of woods, while weapons consisted of a sword,

40

VIKING HERSIR

knife, and possibly a pair of short javelins. However, the most feared Viking weapon was the single or two-handed ax. This, swung in great arcs, could cause horrific, invariably fatal, wounds

The Vikings may have used horses to travel overland during their raids but invariably fought on foot when taking part in a major battle. Prior to combat, the Vikings would form up into a shield wall, a dense, closely-packed body of men up to five or so ranks deep and the hersirs themselves usually fought in the front ranks. Within the wall itself, men armed with swords and axes would make up the front ranks, followed by spearmen. The rear ranks comprised slingers, bowmen, and men with javelins. Although a single block of men was usual, contemporary records indicate that two or more might be formed if the raiding party was large enough. Occasionally, a force might be held in reserve.

There was one noteworthy variation to the flat-fronted shield wall, which was known as the "Svynfylking." This consisted of a wedge-like formation with the pointed end facing the enemy. If there were sufficient Vikings to form several wedges, they would form up side by side thereby creating a zigzagging line. The tactics of the Vikings relied on their fighting skills and fearsome reputation. Against a dismounted enemy, battle would begin with the slingers, archers, and javelineers using their weapons to create holes in the enemy's front line. Next, the opposing front ranks would fight at close range. Vikings are believed to have been much less successful against cavalry. For example, fighting against the mounted Franks at the Battle of Saucourt in 881, they suffered losses totaling 8,000 men.

Despite their reputation, the Vikings were not invincible. In the campaign against the English Saxon King Harold in 1066, they won a great victory at Gate Fulford but were then virtually wiped out at the Battle of Stamford Bridge. Ironically, Harold's Saxons were then crushed at the Battle of Hastings by the Normans, themselves of Viking origin.

FACT BOX

NATIONALITY **SCANDINAVIAN**
LOCATION **EUROPE**

CAMPAIGNS
Sea-going raiders/1066 invasion of England

TYPE: **INFANTRY**

FACTFINDER GUIDE: **WARRIORS**

Norman Knight

11TH CENTURY

The Normans, descendants of Vikings from Scandinavia who had settled in north France, developed the finest heavy cavalry of the early Middle Ages. Details of their clothing, weapons, equipment, and tactics have been taken from the famous Bayeux Tapestry, which recounts the story of William the Conqueror's successful invasion of England in 1066.

Norman knights wore a knee-length "hauberk" (shirt) of chainmail, which was slashed to the hips front and rear so that the knight could mount and ride his highly trained and valuable warhorse, while their lower legs were covered in woollen leggings, usually tightly bound with leather straps. The warrior's shoes were also made of leather and had a simple metal spur. The sleeves of the hauberk reached to the elbow. A knight's head and neck was protected by a chainmail "coif" (close-fitting hood), usually attached to the hauberk, although some knights are shown with a leather hood. A helmet was also worn, and this was of a conical metal design fitted with a broad nasal guard to protect the nose from sword or ax cuts.

A knight's weapons consisted of a long, tapering sword, which was primarily used for slashing rather than thrusting at a target. The sword was protected in a leather scabbard, sometimes hanging from a shoulder or waist belt, but on occasion thrust through a slit made in the hauberk so that only the sword's hilt could be seen. The knight's chief weapon was, however, the lance. This was usually eight or nine feet long and topped by a metal point. The Bayeux Tapestry shows lances adorned with colorful pennants, but it is not known if these were purely for ornamentation or identification, or marked an early form of heraldry. A knight was also equipped with a long wooden kite-shaped shield. This was probably faced with leather or thin sheets of metal, and many had a raised central metal boss. Worn on the left arm, shields were usually decorated with a variety of colored motifs; crosses and mythical animals were particularly popular.

The key tactic of the Norman knight was the close-order charge delivered at thunderous speed. Although there is evidence that the lance was occasionally thrown at an enemy, it was primarily a shock weapon in the charge. A knight would level his spear under his right arm and use the weight of man and horse traveling at speed to crash through an enemy formation. The shock of a Norman charge was so great because of three advances in military technology. First, a Norman saddle was high at the back and front, enabling a knight to keep his seat. Second, stirrups allowed him to control and direct his mount, and also keep his seat. Third, Norman warhorses had horseshoes, which made them more sure-footed and able to build up greater speed during a charge.

The greatest victory won by the Norman knight was the Battle of Hastings in 1066. This was a long, hard-fought battle between William the Conqueror and England's Saxon king, Harold. When it ended Harold was dead and his army crushed. On Christmas Day, William was crowned as in London's Westminster Abbey as William I. That his conquest of England had been so rapid and successful was in no small part due to the fighting skills of his armored knights.

NORMAN HEAVY CAVALRYMAN.

FACT BOX

NATIONALITY **FRENCH**
LOCATION **EUROPE**

CAMPAIGNS
Various campaigns in Europe including the 1066 invasion and subjugation of England

TYPE: **CAVALRY**

43

FACTFINDER GUIDE: **WARRIORS**

Crusader Knight

12TH CENTURY

CRUSADER KNIGHTS WRESTED THE HOLY LAND FROM THE SARACENS DURING THE FIRST CRUSADE.

At the end of the 11th century, Christian Europe embarked on a series of Crusades to recapture the Holy Land, especially Jerusalem, from the Muslims. There were four Crusades between 1096 and 1204, but the first from a Christian point of view was the most successful and resulted in the capture of Jerusalem and the creation of four Christian states in the Holy Land. With the Holy Land and Jerusalem now open to Christian pilgrims, it became essential that the pilgrim routes be protected and various military-religious orders of knight were created.

Among these brotherhoods were Knights Templar, who were founded in 1115 to escort pilgrims. The Templars were truly religious—they vowed to live a life of poverty and committed themselves to a life of religious observance. They also swore to fight non-Christians whatever the odds against them, refuse to be ransomed if captured, and die for the Christian cause if necessary. By the second half of the 12th century the Templars wielded enormous power and only by the end of the century were they rivaled in power, by the Knights of St. John of Jerusalem. Another famous

CRUSADER KNIGHT

sect was the Order of Teutonic Knights of the Hospital of St. Mary the Virgin, which was founded during the siege of Acre in 1090.

The knights of the religious orders were not dressed or equipped and did not fight in any way differently from other knights. They wore three-quarter length chain-mail shirts and chain-mail leggings. Helmets, under which a mail covering was worn, were conical in the Norman style or, increasingly as time passed, had a flat top without the nasal bar. Over the armor, the knights would were a long flowing sleeveless coat known as a "surtout." The various orders had surtouts of various colors, usually with a Christian cross. The Teutonic knights, for example, wore white surtouts emblazoned with black crosses. Their weapons consisted of the lance, usually between ten and 12 feet long and a sword up to around 30 inches in length. Axes and maces were also popular weapons.

The various orders were particularly renowned as castle-builders. They had the wealth and resources to build huge fortifications, which acted as their bases and headquarters, as well as places of refuge during times of unrest. The castles also acted as stopping-off points for pilgrims on their way to various holy sites and dominated the surrounding countryside. Perhaps the most famous castle was the Krak des Chevaliers, widely considered to be the strongest fortification in the world at the time.

The Holy Land was eventually lost to the Crusaders at the end of the 13th century. Even the supposedly invunerable Krak des Chevaliers was captured in 1271, but the religious orders continued to fight to preserve and expand Christian Europe. Some orders returned to their homelands, where most held extensive estates while others occupied islands in the Mediterranean, most notably Rhodes and Malta, from where they struggled to prevent the expansion of the Muslim world with varying degrees of success.

THE CRUSADER'S ADVERSARIES WOULD REGAIN THEIR LOST LANDS AND HOLD THEM DESPITE FURTHER CRUSADES.

FACT BOX

NATIONALITY	**EUROPEAN CHRISTIANS**
LOCATION	**HOLY LAND**

CAMPAIGNS
The Crusades

TYPE: **CAVALRY**

FACTFINDER GUIDE: **WARRIORS**

Mongol Cavalryman

EARLY 13TH CENTURY

MONGOL HORSEMAN ARMED WITH BOW.

Under Genghis Khan (1162-1227) and his successors, the Mongols of central Asia carved out one of history's great empires, which at its height stretched from China to the frontier of Eastern Europe. The ferociousness of their many campaigns and their seeming invincibility made the Mongols greatly feared by those they sought to conquer. It was not unusual for Mongols, who became experts at siege warfare, to slaughter all the inhabitants of a city that had defied them once it had been captured. Despite what their contemporaries said, Mongol armies, though large, were not always stronger than those of their opponents. However, they were almost invariably better trained, led, and organized. For example, the later Mongol armies that cut a swathe through Russia, Eastern, and Central Europe never exceeded more than around 150,000 men.

The vast majority of any Mongol forces were highly trained, disciplined cavalrymen—around 40 percent of a field force would consist of heavy cavalry. These warriors wore armor, usually of leather although sometimes of chainmail taken from a fallen enemy, and their principal weapon was the lance. The remainder of a Mongol force comprised highly mobile light cavalry. These wore no armor and were armed with a powerful bow (and a plentiful supply of arrows), javelins, and a lasso. Both types carried axes or curved swords. It was the combination of these two types of cavalry acting in

MONGOL CAVALRYMAN

coordination, both on campaign and in battle, that made the Mongols virtually invincible.

Mongol armies were organized on the decimal system. The largest unit was the "touman" with 10,000 men divided between 10 regiments of 1,000. Each regiment had ten squadrons of ten troops, each of 10 men. Three or more toumans made up an army. These units, and all others, were officered by men who had been selected for their leadership abilities or bravery in battle. On campaign each Mongol column was accompanied by thousands of spare horses, one for each man, so that when one horse was exhausted it could be replaced by a fresher mount. Mongol armies usually advanced at great speed on a broad front, screened by light cavalry who scouted ahead. Once an enemy had been sighted the various toumens could combine quickly in overwhelming strength.

Mongol battle tactics relied on the interplay between their two types of cavalry. Before a battle, they would form up in five widely spaced lines with heavy cavalry filling the first two. As the enemy drew near, the rear three ranks of light cavalry would advance to bow range and shower the opposing ranks with volleys of arrows or javelins. Often this was enough to shatter a foe, but if it was not, the heavy cavalry would launch a devastating charge. Few of the Mongols' opponents could stand up to this combination of firepower and shock action. The martial abilities of the Mongols can be judged by their invasion of central Europe in 1241. Under Subotai, some 120,000 Mongols, split between four armies, each of three toumans, moved into what are now Hungary and Poland. The decisive battle took place at the Savo River on April 11. Although outnumbered by the 100,000 Hungarians present, Subotai's force crushed their opponents. Estimates of the Hungarian dead range from 40,000 to 70,000.

FACT BOX

NATIONALITY **MONGOL**
LOCATION **CENTRAL ASIA**

CAMPAIGNS
Numerous wars of conquest, 12th-15th centuries

TYPE: **CAVALRY**

FACTFINDER GUIDE: **WARRIORS**

English Longbowman

EARLY 15TH CENTURY

THE LONGBOW CHANGED THE BATTLEFIELD. FAR RIGHT: ENGLAND BATTLES FRANCE AT CRECY.

The English longbow was the weapon that effectively ended the battlefield dominance of the mounted armored knight in the late Middle Ages. In three decisive victories during the Hundred Years War—Crecy (1346), Poitiers (1356), and Agincourt (1415)—longbowmen were able to inflict horrific casualties on the flower of France's nobility. Their victories signalled that the supposedly humble foot soldiers would become the dominant battlefield soldier.

The longbow originated in Wales and was between five and six feet in length. Several different types of wood were used for the bow staves, but yew was the preferred material. Arrows were usually three feet long and fitted with a variety of heads. One, known as the "bodkin," consisted of a square tip ending in a chisel-like point; it was specifically designed to penetrate chainmail at long range and even plate armor at closer range. A skilled archer could fire arrows out to a distance of around 300.

Longbowmen wore little or no armor, possibly aside from a helmet and a little chainmail to protect the head and they often took items from the bodies of enemy dead if it was more up to date. Other clothing might consist of woollen leggings and quilted jackets. Many wore emblems or colors that identified them as retainers of a particular member of the nobility, although the English red cross became increasingly popular. Some might also carry a small shield known as a buckler for protection in close-quarter combat.

48

ENGLISH LONGBOWMAN

On campaign, English archers could amount to 80 percent of the army with the remainder made up of knights and men-at-arms. In battle, both types would fight on foot, often behind field defenses such as rows of stakes or potholes. Both of these were designed to break up any charge by the enemy cavalry. The standard battle formation comprised wedges of longbowmen separated by blocks of knights and men-at-arms.

The English fought defensive battles, rightly believing that the impetuous French knights could be relied upon to made a headlong charge during which the longbow could be used to devastating effect. The weapon itself was reasonably accurate but its great strength was the volume of fire skilled longbowmen could unleash on an approaching enemy, with six or more arrows a minute being not uncommon. Knights were killed or wounded by this fire and their wounded horses would also become unmanageable, further breaking up the cohesion of the charge. Few knights reached the English lines.

Those knights who did manage to reach the English would be halted by stakes and potholes. They and their horses might be wounded, and all would be exhausted. The English, both bowmen and infantry, now sallied out from behind their defenses, surrounding individual knights. The archers would abandon their bows and use other weapons—swords, mallets, and knives, to attack knights who were pulled from their horses and blundered around in heavy armor—easy meat for a lightly equipped bowman.

The longbow had one main drawback. To use it effectively required long periods of practise. To become fully proficient took years not weeks or months. In the latter stages of the Hundred Years War, the French also began to develop tactics to defeat the English. First, they encouraged the English to attack them, thereby making the lightly-equipped longbowmen more vulnerable, Second, they began to use artillery and early firearms to blast the English ranks as they advanced. The importance of the longbow declined as gunpowder weapons become more reliable and effective.

FACT BOX

NATIONALITY	**ENGLISH**
LOCATION	**WESTERN EUROPE**

CAMPAIGNS
Welsh and Scottish Wars, Hundred Years War, Wars of the Roses, Burgundian Wars

TYPE: **MISSLE-ARMED LIGHT INFANTRY**

FACTFINDER GUIDE: **WARRIORS**

French Knight

EARLY 15TH CENTURY

A FRENCH KNIGHT WITH SHIELD AND LANCE.

Although French armies in many of the major battles of the Hundred Years War (1337-1453) against England were large, the bulk of them consisted of poorly trained city militias and virtually untrained peasants. The cutting edge of the French forces were the armored lords, knights, and their retainers. These usually, but by no means exclusively, fought on horseback.

Although armor was constantly evolving and being refined, the best-equipped knights in the first decades of the 15th century were encased from head to foot in plate armor, with the joints protected by chainmail that allowed the elbows and knees to move freely. Full plate armor consisted of a large number of metal sheets that were cut or molded to fit the body. A shield was worn on the left arm and was often concave in shape to deflect lance hits away from the body. However, because plate armor offered excellent protection against sword cuts and the like, shields were slowly disappearing from the battlefield. A Knight's weapons consisted of the lance, which was couched underarm during a charge, and a variety of cutting or thrusting weapons, chiefly the sword and ax.

The standard tactic of the armored knight was the charge. Large numbers of knights and their retainers would form up in a tightly packed mass and then launch themselves against the enemy line. It was generally believed

FRENCH KNIGHT

that the sight and sound of such a force would compel the enemy's humble infantry to flee the battlefield. If this did not happen, the knights would use their weight, speed, and force to punch a wedge through the enemy line. The knights would then seek out those of equal rank, who they would engage in hand-to-hand combat to gain prestige and honor. Traditional battles between knights could often degenerate into a series of individual combats, thereby making it virtually impossible for a commander to coordinate his forces.

The main problem with the charge of a body of knights was that it was rarely delivered at full speed, but rather at a trot—the weight of the fully-armed and armored knight, and the difficulties of maintaining formation at speed, made the full-blooded charge difficult to achieve. Terrain could also conspire against the charge. At the Battle of Agincourt in 1415, for example, the French advance against the English was slowed by a muddy, rain-drenched plowed field. Equally, there was little finesse in a charge. Once one had begun, knights rarely changed direction or maneuvered to gain an advantage; their main role was to get to grips with the enemy as quickly as possible.

To make matters worse, although plate armor was nowhere near as heavy or constricting as has previously been believed, it could still cause difficulties in close combat. Visored helmets restricted a knight's vision and the knight could not fight for long without tiring. If a knight was dismounted, thus losing the mobility of being on horseback, and forced to fight more mobile troops, he was put at a considerable disadvantage. Isolated, tired, and disorganized knights were much more easy to deal with. Agincourt clearly demonstrated the weakness of the French knights—their attack was ill-coordinated, became bogged down in the morass, and was shot to pieces by the English archers. Some 5,000 knights of all ranks were killed and a further 1,000 captured.

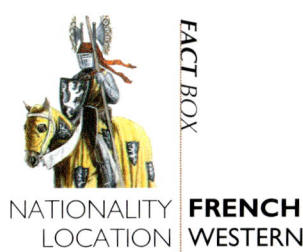

FACT BOX

NATIONALITY **FRENCH**
LOCATION **WESTERN EUROPE**

CAMPAIGNS
Later stages of the Hundred Years War

TYPE: **HEAVY CAVALRY**

FACTFINDER GUIDE: **WARRIORS**

Hussite Infantry

EARLY 15TH CENTURY

HUSSITE WAGON CASTLE OR DEFENSIVE LAGER OF THE 15th CENTURY.

The Hussites were a religious sect based in Bohemia, who were persecuted for their views and their desire to establish a homeland independent of German rule. The Hussite leader, Jan Hus, was arrested and then burnt to death by the German emperor in 1415, an event that sparked intermittent wars between 1419 and 1436. However, the Hussites were not soldiers and seemed to have little chance of defeating the knight-led armies of the Germans. Nevertheless, the new Hussite leader, Jan Zizka, developed weapons and tactics to defeat the flower of German chivalry.

Zizka, although he insisted on regular training for the Hussites, realized that they would stand little chance in the open against knights, so he developed the idea of the "wagenburg," a mobile fortress made from modified wagons. Using farm wagons pulled by four or more horses and fitted with large shields or loopholed boards, he decided to attack the Germans. His column of wagons would advance into enemy territory and shortly before

52

HUSSITE INFANTRY

battle began they would form into a square or circle, with the wagons secured by chains and the gaps between the protected by wooden palisades. The horse teams would be sheltered in the center of the wagenburg.

As the Germans cavalry discovered, the wagons were difficult to attack. They were filled with infantry who were protected behind their wooden defenses. The infantry were of several types. Regulations specified that each wagon was to be filled with two handgunners (handguns were early gunpowder weapons) six crossbowmen, 14 men equipped with flails (agricultural implements used to separate wheat from chaff) and four halberdiers. Other Hussites carried heavy wooden clubs fitted with spikes. As the Hussite Wars progressed, the proportion of handgunners increased and early types of cannon were taken on campaign. These were mounted on carriages and protected by a wooden palisade.

The Hussite battle tactics were straightforward. Attacking knights would be blasted by the handgunners, crossbowmen, and cannon. Those who managed to reach the wagenburg would then be cut down or pulled from their horses by the troops equipped by the flails or halberdiers. If the enemy attack showed signs of failing, then the Hussites' own cavalry would sally out from inside the wagenburg to complete their destruction.

The Hussites, who were usually outnumbered, became so successful that they even took the fight to their enemies. Such campaigns usually involved them advancing into enemy territory and then forming their wagenburg to wait for the Germans to attack on unfavorable terms. However, the Hussite system of war had one particular shortcoming—it needed huge numbers of horses, which were often in short supply. Nevertheless, the Hussites proved that the mounted knight could be defeated by infantry. The Hussites were almost unique in the use of the wagenburg, and their experiments of combining mobility and warfare in such an unusual way did not survive the end of their wars for religious and political freedom.

FACT BOX

NATIONALITY **CZECHOSLOVAKIAN**
LOCATION **CENTRAL EUROPE**

CAMPAIGNS
Religious wars (1419-36)

TYPE: **INFANTRY**

FACTFINDER GUIDE: **WARRIORS**

Swiss Pikeman

EARLY 16TH CENTURY

THE PIKE DOMINATED THE 15th CENTURY BATTLEFIELD.

Swiss infantry, predominantly pikemen, were the most successful infantry of the late 15th and early 16th centuries. The first earned their reputation of virtual invincibility in a series of crushing victories against Burgundy's Charles the Bold in the 1470s. Later, the Swiss begin the supreme mercenaries of Western Europe, hiring themselves out to the highest bidder. Their battlefield dominance lasted until the second decade of the 16th century, when the introduction of well-trained early musketeers, usually fighting from behind field defenses, ended their reign. For over 50 years, the Swiss were rarely defeated. They were renowned and feared for their training, courage, and ferocity and rarely took prisoners.

In their early battles the Swiss were equipped with eight foot halberds but these were gradually replaced with pikes, which eventually reached a length of 18 feet. In action, the Swiss pikemen formed up in dense, deep blocks. Although the number of blocks could vary, there were usually three,

SWISS PIKEMAN

positioned one behind the other. The leading block was known as the "Vorhut," the middle was the "Gewaltschaufen," and the rear block was the "Nachhut." These might be of equal or different strengths.

At the Battle of Novara (1513) in the French and Italian Wars, for example, the main block contained 6,000 men and was supported by two other blocks of 1,000 and 2,000 pikemen.

The blocks might be preceded by missile troops and cannon to soften up the enemy. At first crossbowmen were deployed but these were replaced by early musketeers, and a few cavalrymen might protect the wings of the pikeblocks. However, early Swiss armies consisted of anything up to 90 percent pikemen, a figure that declined slowly to a total of around 75 percent.

The Swiss pikeblocks had a very simple tactic. On spotting the enemy, even if heavily outnumbered, they attacked immediately. The blocks could move at incredible speed, which often gave them an element of surprise. The pikemen wielded their weapons at head height, with the point sloping slightly downward. Their momentum would often allow them to crash through an enemy formation, thereby destroying its cohesion. As the enemy broke and fled, they were cut down—battles involving the Swiss were noteworthy for their bloodthirstiness.

Apart from those men in the front ranks of a pikeblock, the Swiss did not wear body armor, though most would have been equipped with a helmet. Clothing was simple, consisting of tight fitting leggings and tunics. These might be of a single color or multi-colored, and often carried a white cross, the Swiss national emblem. However, legend suggests that their clothing was so badly torn after their victory over Charles the Bold at Grandson in 1476, that the Swiss tore clothing from their dead enemies to patch their clothes. This slashed, multi-colored clothing became extremely popular and was copied by many of their own enemies, chiefly the German "Landsknechts" who fought in a similar fashion to the Swiss.

FACT BOX

NATIONALITY **SWISS**
LOCATION **WESTERN EUROPE**

CAMPAIGNS
Burgundian Wars, French and Italian Wars

TYPE: **HEAVY INFANTRY**

FACTFINDER GUIDE: **WARRIORS**

German Reiter

LATE 16TH CENTURY

THE CARCOLE IN ACTION DURING THE FRENCH WARS OF RELIGION.

The German word "reiter" means rider and refers to an early experiment to marry the mobility of cavalry with the firepower of the wheel-lock pistol, the first effective firearm that was small enough to be used in action by a mounted soldier. Although the reiters initially carried lances and swords, the lances were gradually replaced by the pistols during the 16th century. Reiters primarily fought as mercenaries, hiring themselves to various European monarchies at a time when there were few professional armies

Reiters initially wore armor, although their horses were unarmored. By the mid-16th century this armor would generally consist of back and breastplates and an open-faced helmet. Armor was often blackened as a means of preventing rust, but this also led to the reiters being nicknamed "Black Reiters." To the French, probably because of their reputation, they were known as the "Black Devils." They usually carried two pistols, which were placed in holsters attached to the saddle. Evidence also indicates that some might carry a third tucked into the right boot.

Although the strength of reiter forces varied, the basic unit was a

GERMAN REITER

squadron of between 300 and 350 cavalrymen. In battle, these squadrons would form up in close order in blocks 10 or so ranks deep. The reason for this depth was that in their favored tactic of firing rank by rank, one after the other, the reiters needed time to reload their weapons. Only after an enemy unit had been "shot up" by successive volleys would the reiters charge with their swords drawn. Sometimes used as an additional weapon, the long wheel-lock pistols could be held by the barrel and the rounded butt used as a club.

Their chief tactic of the reiters was the "caracole." Formed up in their deep blocks, they would advance at the trot on an enemy unit until they were in pistol range. The front rank of reiters would then discharge their pistols and then retire to the rear rank to reload, while the reiters in the other ranks would successively fire their weapons. In effect, the enemy had to face a constant barrage of pistol balls. If successful, a caracole could cut swathes through densely packed ranks of infantry.

However, although some where impressed by the effectiveness of the caracole, notably the French during their Wars of Religion (1562-68), it had several shortcomings. First, it demanded that the reiters were superbly trained and disciplined, because of its complexity. Second, while carrying out the caracole, the reiters were vulnerable to sudden attack by enemy cavalry forces as they carried out their complicated maneuvers. Thirdly, and most damagingly, the effectiveness of the caracole itself was totally undermined by improvements in the firepower of infantry. Equipped with muskets that could easily outrange the wheel-locks carried by the reiters, the caracole could be shot to pieces at ranges beyond the range of the cavalrymen's weapons. Even if an enemy unit suffered casualties, its pikemen could keep the reiters from getting to grips with their swords because of their greater reach.

FACT BOX

NATIONALITY: **GERMAN**
LOCATION: **WESTERN EUROPE**

CAMPAIGNS
Various 16th century wars

TYPE: **MEDIUM CAVALRY**

FACTFINDER GUIDE: **WARRIORS**

Spanish Infantry

16TH AND 17TH CENTURIES

SPANISH "TERCIOS" WERE LARGE INFANTRY UNITS.

Once the Spanish has evicted the Muslim Moors from Spain in the late 15th century, they embarked on a succession of military adventures that would gain them territories in Northern Europe and elsewhere. The Spanish quickly established themselves as among the best and most disciplined soldiers in the world, evolving a military system that became the model for later permanent units of troops.

During the mid-1500s, the Spanish radically overhauled the structure and organization of the forces. The central part of this policy being the establishment of "tercios." These were large infantry units that were kept together for both administrative and tactical purposes. The ranks of each tercio were filled with men from a particular region controlled by Spain. Tercios were formed from existing units, known as "corunelas," each of which, in the early 1500s, consisted of between 1,000 and 1,500 men. Corunelas were commanded by "coronels," which is the origin of the modern rank of colonel, the commander of a regiment. The troops of a ter-

SPANISH INFANTRY

cio were split between 12 companies of around 250 men.

A typical tercio contained a variety of troop types. Two of the companies were wholly equipped with "arquebuses" (early muskets), while the others were a 50-50 mix of arquebusiers and pikemen. As the century progressed the number of arquebusiers increased and the arquebus was replaced by more effective muskets. In battle, the tercios various troops types formed up in a particular formation. This consisted of a central block of pikemen, who were used to shelter the infantry if they were charged by cavalry, with the arquebusiers or musketeers arranged outside the pike block. Four blocks of these were formed at the corners of the pike block and these were linked by a thin screen of similarly armed troops.

The great strength of the tercio in battle was that it was organized to give all-round protection. Unlike infantry in line or column, it had no open flanks or rear, which could be attacked by cavalry and the infantry equipped with firearms could shelter behind the pikes while they reloaded. However, the tercio did have its weaknesses. It was not very mobile as it was difficult to maintain order in such a formation, it was wasteful of firepower as only some of the arquebusiers or musketeers could fire on any one target coming from a particular direction, and it was a large and tempting target for enemy artillery. To offset the dangers of artillery fire, tercios were often placed behind field fortifications.

The tercio showed its worth in many battles, such as the Garigliano River in 1503, where the Spanish commander Hernandez de Cordoba crushed a joint French-Italian army, and at Biccoca (1522) and Pavia (1525). However, the inflexibility of the tercio was shown during the Thirty Years' War (1618-48). At the Battle of Rocroi on May 19, 1643, a French army commanded by Duke Louis d'Enghien used massed artillery fire to smash the Spanish tercios. The Spanish army had 8,000 men killed and 7,000 captured. The era of the tercio was over but it had been responsible for developing the concept of the permanent regiment that was to become the norm.

FACT BOX

NATIONALITY **SPANISH**
LOCATION **EUROPE**

CAMPAIGNS
Various 16th and 17th century wars

TYPE: **INFANTRY**

FACTFINDER GUIDE: **WARRIORS**

Ottoman Janissary

LATE 16TH CENTURY

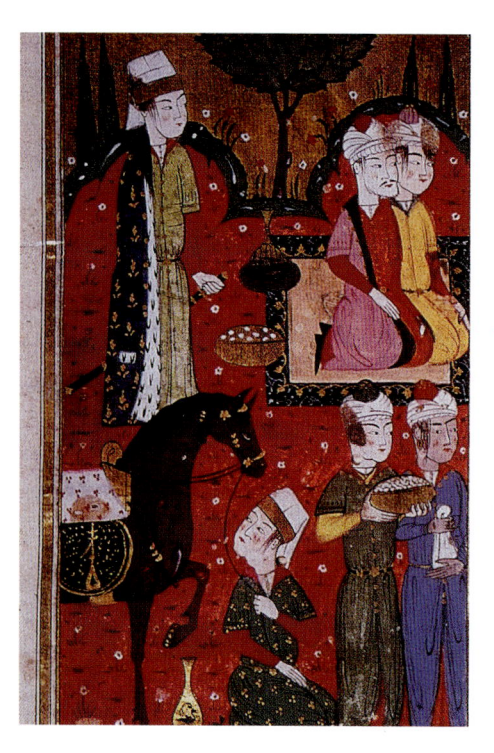

THE OTTOMANS RULED FROM MORDERN-DAY ISTANBUL.

The Ottomans carved out a great Muslim empire, based in Constantinople (now Istanbul in Turkey), which they captured from the Byzantines in 1453, and came to dominate much of the Middle East and the Balkans. They reached the height of their power under Suleiman the Magnificent, who ruled from 1520 to 1566. Ottoman armies were huge, but the majority were poorly trained levies (conscripted troops). However, their forces had a tough, professional core, including artillery and certain cavalry units, but the most famous Ottoman soldiers were the Janissaries.

Founded in 1362, the ranks of the Janissaries, which means "new soldiers," were originally filled with men who had been born Christian. Many were captured in Ottoman raids. Others, when young, had been taken from non-Muslim families in regions conquered by the Ottomans under a tribute system known as "devschirme," and then raised to maturity in the Muslim faith. They were stationed at the heart of the Muslim court and had a major influence on politics. Janissaries were organized in "ortas," which varied in strength from 100 to over 2,500 men. At the height of their

60

OTTOMAN JANISSARY

power, the Janissaries were formed in 101 ortas—Suleiman could call on 12,000 of them.

Unlike many soldiers of the period, the Janissaries were full-time professionals. All were schooled in various military skills and examinations selected those destined to become officers or achieve even higher office. After training, Janissaries lived in barracks and even received regular pay. There were also financial benefits for old or disabled members of the ranks.

The Janissaries were originally equipped with bows, crossbows, and javelins, but these were superseded by early muskets in the 16th century. They were renowned for their colorful, flamboyant uniforms, which consisted of a short-sleeved, flowing, ankle-length coat over a long-sleeved tunic. The coat was often turned up at the front and tucked into a sash or held in place with buttons. On parade, a tall, usually white, felt hat with plumes was worn.

In battle the Janissaries literally formed the core of an Ottoman army, being placed in the center and often surrounded by wagons or cannon chained together to protect them from cavalry charges. Because of their training and strict discipline, the Janissaries were generally superior to any infantry they might face.

The strengths and weaknesses of the Janissaries were closely linked to the rise and fall of the Ottoman Empire. The capture of Constantinople, considered to be the most heavily defended city in the world at the time, was finally achieved after a long siege when Janissaries stormed its walls. But It can be argued the watering down of the Janissaries with the influx of those not born Christian in later centuries and the growing involvement in politics rather than military matters may have played some part in Ottoman defeats at the naval Battle of Lepanto (1571) and the defeat outside Vienna in 1683, two serious reverses which effectively halted Ottoman expansion into the eastern Mediterranean and Southern Europe.

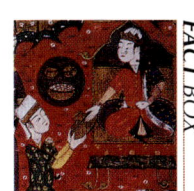

FACT BOX

NATIONALITY	**OTTOMAN TURKISH**
LOCATION	**MIDDLE EAST, EASTERN MEDITERRANEAN, AND BALKANS**

CAMPAIGNS
Throughout the empire

TYPE: **INFANTRY**

FACTFINDER GUIDE: **WARRIORS**

Samurai Warrior

16TH CENTURY

THE JAPANESE SAMURAI FOLLOWED A STRICT COD OF HONOR.

The origins of Japan's samurai warrior caste are unclear but they probably emerged at sometime in the Heian Period between 794 and 1185. The earliest samurai were smaller landowners who allied themselves with one or other of Japan's powerful regional warlords. In return for the lord's protection and support, the samurai swore an oath of loyalty and offered him their military services.

The samurai wore various types of protection, which by the late 16th century consisted of a type of lacquered body armor known as "yukinoshita-do," which included a solid chest protector that was considered safe against arquebus balls. The head was protected by an open front rounded helmet known as a "zunari-kabuto." Before a battle, samurai might also wear a personal banner, which was fixed to a socket on the back of his armor, but once the fighting had begun, the banner was usually held by a retainer. The samurai's chief weapon was a long,

SAMURAI WARRIOR

curved sword with a high-quality blade, known as the "katana."

Samurai warfare was, at least to begin with, highly ritualized. The warrior code—"bushido"—demanded that samurai had to seek out rival samurai in battle and engage in personal combat. Before a battle, individual samurai might call out their name, family, and military exploits to identify themselves to an enemy of sufficiently equal rank. Death in battle was considered more honorable than capture, and a samurai was expected to die in battle if his lord was killed.

The first samurai became embroiled in numerous civil wars, such as the Gempei Wars of the late 12th century, but Japan itself was twice threatened by Mongol invasion in the latter part of the following century. The Mongols were defeated on both occasions and, although the samurai fought well, the outcome of each invasion was decided by typhoons, which swept away the invasion fleets. The winds, known as "kamikaze," were considered to reflect divine intervention.

After the defeat of the Mongols, samurai were involved in a long period of civil wars as rival warlords fought to gain authority over Japan. The samurai way of life—elaborate rituals in which divine significance was given to the warrior's sword, was now threatened by technology. New types of infantry, from the peasant classes and known as "ashigaru," began to be equipped with early firearms.

At the Battle of Nagashino in 1575, two rival warlords clashed. Takeda Katsuyori launched his forces against those commanded by Oda Nobunaga. To offset the Takeda cavalry, Nobunaga deployed 3,000 of his best arquebusiers behind a palisade. They shot the horse-mounted samurai to pieces. Although the samurai would, in various forms, continue to dominate Japanese society and politics for centuries, Nagashino showed clearly that the old system of ritualized warfare could not survive in the face of gunpowder weapons. Subsequently, the samurai increasingly took on the role of officers in command of the ashigaru, although the sword remained the symbol of the warrior and lent him his authority. Samurai were not officially abolished until the Meiji Restoration in 1868.

FACT BOX

NATIONALITY **JAPANESE**
LOCATION **JAPAN**

CAMPAIGNS
Various Japanese civil wars; 13th century Mongol invasions of Japan

TYPE: **INFANTRY**

FACTFINDER GUIDE: **WARRIORS**

Royalist Cavalryman

MID 17TH CENTURY

A 17th CENTURY CAVALRY MELEE.

Those who supported King Charles against Parliament during the English Civil War (1642-46) were known as Royalists. At the beginning of the war, England had little in the way of a standing professional army, but Charles was able to draw on wealthy subjects who were willing to raise and equip units whose ranks were filled by their own retainers and servants. The best of these were the cavalry, who proved more than a match for Parliament's mounted forces for much of the war, particularly when commanded by such a charismatic and experienced leader as the king's nephew, Prince Rupert.

The weapons and tactics of the Royalist cavalry were almost directly copied from the rest of Europe, where Rupert and other officers had seen extensive military service. Cavalry regiments had a theoretical strength of around 500 men, divided between squadrons and troops, but few regiments were this strong on active service. In battle, the most flexible unit was the squadron of around 100 men.

A typical cavalryman wore a metal breastplate to protect the front of his

ROYALIST CAVALRYMAN

upper body and occasionally a backplate as well. Under this might be a leather jerkin that was tough enough to protect the wearer from sword cuts. Long leather boots, often turned down, and leather gauntlets were also worn and the head was often protected by a metal helmet ("lobsterpot"), often fitted with an broad "tail" to protect the neck and three-bars to protect the face. Alternatively, a metal skull cap might be worn under a broad-brimmed felt hat.

The weapons carried by a cavalryman of the time were fairly standardized, consisting of a long, straight sword, which could be used for both cutting and thrusting, and a pair of wheel-lock pistols. Some men, usually officers, might also have carried short axes, but these were rare and probably acted as a badge of rank.

In the early part of the war, Royalist cavalry regiments drew up by squadron in three ranks, although the number of ranks was gradually increased to provide greater shock during a charge. Attacks on the enemy were usually made at the gallop with swords drawn. Pistols might be fired in close-combat with other cavalry or used to shoot gaps in the ranks of infantry through which the Royalist cavalry could charge.

In many battles of the Civil War, a strong Royalist cavalry charge was usually enough to sweep the Parliamentary cavalry from the battlefield. However, the Royalist regiments were plagued by a lack of discipline and would often pursue their defeated foe for miles, thereby playing little or no further part in the battle. Ideally, they should have halted their charge, reformed, and then launched other attacks against enemy regiments. This problem became apparent at the Edgehill, the first major battle of the war, and was never fully addressed. This was to have fatal consequences for the Royalist cause. At the Battle of Naseby in 1645, the war's decisive engagement, Royalist cavalry smashed the cavalry on one wing of the Parliamentary army, but then disappeared to attack the enemy's baggage train. Parliament's remaining cavalry, highly trained and disciplined due to the efforts of Oliver Cromwell, then helped to crush the remaining parts of the king's army.

FACT BOX

NATIONALITY ENGLISH
LOCATION WESTERN EUROPE

CAMPAIGNS
English Civil War (1642-45)

TYPE: LIGHT CAVALRY

FACTFINDER GUIDE: **WARRIORS**

Cromwellian Musketeer

MID 17TH CENTURY

MUSKETEER CARRYING A MATCHLOCK.

The New Model Army, a force of infantry, cavalry, dragoons, and artillery, was founded in 1644 by senior Parliamentary officers, including Oliver Cromwell, to ensure the defeat of King Charles II's Royalist forces during the latter stages of the English Civil War. It was England's first standing professional army and won the decisive battle of the war, at Naseby, in 1645. It was also involved in later Royalist uprisings and against the Scots, winning great victories at Preston (1648), Dunbar (1650), and Worcester (1651).

At the heart of the New Model Army were 12 infantry regiments with a strength of 1,200 men divided between 10 companies of varying strengths. These companies contained a mix of musketeers and pikemen in the proportion of two-to-one.

Pikemen were becoming of less and less importance in warfare and musketeers were beginning to take on the dominant role. Pikemen were increasingly used to protect the musketeers from cavalry attack as the bayonet had yet to be developed. In battle, the bulk of a regiment's musketeers would form up in ranks six deep on the flanks of its pikemen, although some might be sent forward as skirmishers or to occupy an important piece of ground on the flank.

In the early years of the war, musketeers in the front rank would fire, then move through their colleagues to the rear to reload, while those of the second rank fired. The process continued through the ranks until the first rank again reached the front and was ready to fire. This "countermarch" fire system was slow and cumbersome. The New Model Army's musketeers began to deploy in three ranks and fired by three-rank volleys, which was a much more efficient method of delivering fire.

The clothing of the New Model Army's infantry was standardized, a first in England. Red coats, often with differently colored cuffs to identify a particular regiment, were worn. Unlike pikemen, who wore helmets and upper leg and body armor as protection, musketeers were unprotected, although some may have worn helmets—rather than felt hats or caps—and leather coats that offered some protection against sword cuts.

The weapon carried was the matchlock, in which the gunpowder was ignited by a slow-burning match of rope. It was heavy and most musketeers used a wooden fork on which they rested the barrel of the matchlock as they fired. Muskets were notoriously inaccurate at anything over 150 yards and even the best musketeers were unlikely to fire more than three rounds a minute. Musketeers did fight at close quarters, usually against their enemy counterparts so most carried swords, but their preferred tactic was to hold their muskets by the barrel and wield the wooden stock as a club.

The New Model Army was an outstanding fighting force. Due to its rigorous training (and supposedly regular pay), its soldiers enjoyed high morale and defeated Royalist troops with much more battle experience. However, its creation did more than make sure that Parliament won the English Civil War—it also marked the beginning of the modern British Army.

FACT BOX

NATIONALITY **ENGLISH**
LOCATION **WESTERN EUROPE**

CAMPAIGNS
English Civil War

TYPE: **MUSKET-ARMED INFANTRY**

FACTFINDER GUIDE: **WARRIORS**

American Ranger

MID 18TH CENTURY

MAJOR ROBERT ROGERS.

Between 1756 and 1763, Britain and France, both of who had ambitions to expand their colonial possessions in North America at the expense of the other, fought what became known as the French and Indian War. Both were already engaged against each other in the Seven Years' War and had few troops to spare for distant North America. In consequence they made extensive use of local French-Canadian and American militias, as well as Native Americans. Although the French and British regulars fought some pitched battles, most notably at Quebec in September 1759, where a British victory ended France's power in Canada, the war was dominated by raids, ambushes, and attacks on isolated settlements along the disputed frontier.

European troops were not suited to this type of warfare. Lack of roads made movement difficult, while dense forests and difficult terrain prevented the regulars from fighting in the way they had been trained. The British, like the French, made extensive use of locally raised units, the most famous of which was known as "Rogers' Rangers," named after its commander, Massachusetts-born Robert Rogers (1731-75). The unit, which had reached a strength of nine companies

AMERICAN RANGER

by 1758, had been founded two years earlier. Rogers' own background as a hunter, explorer, and frontiersman reflected the type of recruits who joined the Rangers. Its ranks were filled with frontiersmen—tough, rugged men who had all the hunting and survival skills to take on their French counterparts.

The weapons, equipment, and clothing of the Rangers reflected their role in irregular warfare. Their clothing, sometimes green or black, was hard-wearing and comfortable. Weaponry consisted of muskets or hunting rifles, tomahawks, and knives. Rangers were lightly equipped and their upbringing allowed them to move swiftly and silently through the region's forest. Although they carried some food on their operations, they were equally at home living off the land. Appearing as from nowhere, they proved to be highly skilled at sudden ambushes, attacks on French outposts, and the destruction of Native American villages. In October 1759, for example, they destroyed the village of St. Francis, after a long and difficult cross-country approach.

Rangers did not fight out in the open in the close-packed ranks favored by European regulars. Rather they took advantage of any natural cover. Nor did they fire in mass volleys, preferring to rely on aimed shots. Individual initiative and aggression were prized as much as discipline and the ability to obey orders without question. The French, who could draw on their local militias and Native American allies, initially held the advantage along the disputed frontier, but Ranger units whittled away this advantage as the war progressed.

However, the Rangers also played a key role in the campaigns waged by the regular British forces. For example, Rogers was present at the capture of forts Ticonderoga and Crown Point in 1759 and was again present when Montreal was captured during the following year. In these campaigns, the Rangers acted as scouts and guides for the main force. Although France's North American ambitions were effectively ended by General Wolfe's regular forces at Quebec, the Rangers had ensured that the French raids along the frontier had failed to weaken Britain's grip on its North American colonies.

FACT BOX

NATIONALITY **AMERICAN, EUROPEAN IMMIGRANTS**
LOCATION **NORTH AMERICA**

CAMPAIGNS
French and Indian War (1756-63),
Pontiac's Rebellion (1763),
War of Independence (1775-1783)

TYPE: **LIGHT INFANTRY**

FACTFINDER GUIDE: **WARRIORS**

Highland Clansman

MID 18TH CENTURY

HARSH CLIMACTIC CONDITIONS SHAPED CLANSMEN TACTICS.

On August 19, 1745, Catholic Prince Charles Edward Stuart, the "Young Pretender," raised his standard at Glenfinnan in the far northeast of Scotland. Backed by the French, he was about to embark on a campaign to remove the Protestant English monarchy. It was proclaimed that Charles's father, the "Old Pretender," was the rightful King James VIII of Scotland and III of England, and Charles was nominated his successor. James's supporters were known as "Jacobites" after the Latin for James.

Some, but by no means all, Scots, rallied to Charles's cause—the bulk of the Jacobite forces coming from the Highlands. On the orders of their chieftains and clan leaders, to whom they owed allegiance, some 8,000 Highlanders in total flocked to the cause during the rebellion. They were not professional soldiers, but their harsh and tough way of life had given them certain fighting skills. Those that rallied to the cause tended to fight with members of their own clan, forming "regiments" that might vary in strength from 100 to about 500 men.

Highlanders did not wear military uniforms but went to war in their everyday clothes, such as a tartan plaid (a long length of cloth wrapped

HIGHLAND CLANSMAN

around the waist and then thrown over the shoulder), trews, shirt, waistcoat, and bonnet. The weapons carried by a clansman depended partly on his wealth. Few carried muskets (and the Jacobites were often short of powder and shot) and only the wealthiest might carry a pair of pistols. Most used various cutting weapons, including a broadsword, dirks (short knives) and small shield, or "targe." Other, poorer, clansmen might carry nothing more than a pitchfork or a long-shafted ax.

The tactics of the Highlanders were basic. On sighting the enemy, they would quickly form their clan regiments in one or two lines and then launch a ferocious charge. When within 50 or less yards of the enemy, those that had muskets would discharge and then discard them. As the range fell, pistols would be fired and then thrown at the enemy line. Finally, swords and knives were drawn, and close-quarter battle began, with the Highlanders using their shields to parry bayonet thrusts before cutting and slashing at their shaken opponents. Although unsophisticated, these tactics were sufficient to crush a poor-quality English force at Prestonpans to the east of Edinburgh on September 21, and forced a second English army to retreat after the Battle of Falkirk on February 17, 1746.

The Jacobite Rebellion was destined to fail, however. At the Battle of Culloden on April 16, Charles's much reduced army was crushed. The English commander, the Duke of Cumberland, first used his artillery to kill and disorder the Highland line, which was finally goaded into charging Cumberland's forces. The Jacobites were met by volley after volley of musket fire from well-drilled English (and Scottish) regiments. Some Highlanders did reach the English line and there was a brief flurry of vicious hand-to-hand combat before they were flung back. Charles's army disintegrated and fled. Its destruction signalled the end of Jacobite ambitions and heralded a brutal English campaign of subjugation in the Highlands, which eventually led to the destruction of the Highland way of life and mass emigration of clansmen and their families.

FACT BOX

NATIONALITY SCOTTISH
LOCATION SCOTTISH HIGHLANDS, BRITAIN

CAMPAIGNS
Jacobite Rebellion, 1745-46

TYPE: **INFANTRY**

FACTFINDER GUIDE: **WARRIORS**

Prussian Grenadier

MID 18TH CENTURY

FREDERICK INSPECTING HIS GRENADIERS.

For much of the 18th century there was little to distinguish the armies of Europe's leading powers. They were equipped with similar weapons and fought using much the same tactics on the battlefield. The ordinary infantryman faced severe punishments if he failed to obey orders and was simply expected to follow procedures for moving and firing that had been drummed into him on the parade ground. One general, in the middle of the century, realized that to win battles his infantry had to be superior in the speed and firing to the enemy.

Frederick the Great of Prussia (1712-86) recognized that the average infantry regiment was slow to move and unwieldy, and its soldiers could not fire more than two or three volleys from their flintlock muskets a minute. To make his infantry more effective he had to guarantee that they would follow orders like robots, even in the heat of battle, and thus speed up both their firing and movement. To do this his recruits were drilled endlessly and soldiers were treated with great brutality if they did not learn quickly enough. However, the end product of Frederick's training program were soldiers who were better drilled than any of their rivals. Historians estimate that a Prussian regiment was twice as effective in battle than any enemy unit.

Frederick was almost constantly involved in wars between 1740 and 1763, chiefly the War of the Austrian Succession (1740-48) and the Seven Years War (1756-63). Surrounded by larger hostile neighbors, his plans were based on defeating each in turn before they could unite. His armies moved with incredible speed, sometimes more than 20 miles per day. This speed was matched on the battlefield, where Frederick invariably opted to attack his enemies before they could attack him, believing that the enemy commander would not be able to react to the danger in time by moving his reserves. By rapid movement Frederick could concentrate the bulk of his army against a weak point in the enemy's line.

Frederick's greatest victory was against the Austrians at Leuthen on December 6, 1757. The 65,000 Austrians drew up in a long line on a five-mile front, with their reserves on their right wing. Frederick, with just 33,000 men, made a feint attack against the Austrian's strong right wing, but then, shielded by a range of low hills, turned south and struck rapidly at the enemy's weaker left wing with the bulk of his forces. Supported by artillery fire and cavalry charges, Frederick's infantry sliced through the Austrian line and after hard fighting put the Austrians to flight. Half the Austrian army was killed, wounded, or captured.

Leuthen was a great victory, which clearly demonstrated Frederick's tactical acumen and the quality of his troops. However, it also showed a weakness that would eventually force Frederick to agree peace terms with his enemies. The Prussians suffered over 6,000 casualties at Leuthen, nearly 20 percent of the total committed to battle. Frederick's victories were often costly and Prussia's armies were being bled dry by his constant campaigning. His larger enemies could afford such losses but Prussia could not.

FACT BOX

NATIONALITY **PRUSSIAN**
LOCATION **NORTHERN EUROPE**

CAMPAIGNS
War of the Austrian Succession (1740-48); Seven Years' War (1756-63)

TYPE: **INFANTRY**

FACTFINDER GUIDE: **WARRIORS**

Colonial Minuteman

LATE 18TH CENTURY

THE MINUTEMEN ROSE UP AGAINST BRITISH COLONIAL RULE.

When the American colonies rebelled against Britain's increasingly autocratic and undemocratic rule in 1775, the colonies had no trained standing army. If the colonists were to oppose British rule with force they would, at least until the colonial authorities could agree to form an army, have to rely on semi-trained militias to take on the professional, battle-hardened army of a world power.

A Militia Act introduced in 1775 regularized the colonial militias, calling on all free, able-bodied men aged between 16 and 50 to be formed into companies and regiments officered by local worthies. The act demanded that those enrolled in the militias should make themselves available for periodic training and drill (although these were infrequent and often dispensed with altogether). Most militiamen were local homesteaders and farmers, but some had war experience and many were excellent shots.

The men were to provide their own musket or hunting rifle, sword, bayonet, and other equipment, though many just provided their own firearms. Militiamen wore their own everyday, usually dull-colored clothes, which contrasted sharply with the bright red uniforms of the British. Their terms of service required them to serve without

74

COLONIAL MINUTEMAN

pay for short periods, but only within their own state borders, during times of danger. Because the militias were supposed to be ready for action at a moment's notice, they were known as Minutemen.

The Minutemen could not match the discipline or training of the British Army, whose soldiers fought in close-packed ranks and in which soldiers were expected to follow orders without question. Nor had they much chance of winning a battle in the open against the British, who were more willing to engage in hand-to-hand combat—and were trained to do so at every opportunity. However, as events were to show, the Minuteman did not fight in the traditional manner, which involved trading close-range volleys before launching a bayonet charge. At the Battles of Lexington and Concord on 19 April 1775, Massachusetts militias harried a British column all the way back to Boston. They avoided pitched battle but fought in small groups, moving quickly, and shooting from cover. The British in their bright red uniforms made easy targets. British losses were heavy and the victory did much to stiffen American resolve to oppose the British.

Worse was to follow for the British. Boston was besieged by various militias and a British attempt to break the siege led to the disastrous Battle of Bunker Hill on 17 June. The American militias occupied high ground behind Charleston opposite Boston and built a defensive earthwork overnight. When the British attacked in their dense-packed ranks, they were shot to pieces, losing nearly half of those involved before a last-ditch charge forced the militiamen to retreat. However, the militiamen tightened their grip on Boston and, under the command of General George Washington, forced the British to abandon the city, never to return, on 17 March 1776. The militiamen had won their first great American victory in the War of Independence.

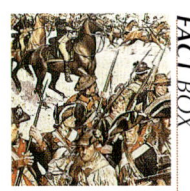

RIGHT: THE BATTLE OF GUILDFORD.

FACT BOX

NATIONALITY **AMERICA**
LOCATION **NORTH AMERICA**

CAMPAIGNS
War of Independence

TYPE: **INFANTRY**

FACTFINDER GUIDE: **WARRIORS**

Continental Infantry

LATE 18TH CENTURY

THE BRITISH ARMY BURN WASHINGTON D.C.

Although the colonial Minutemen had given the British a bloody nose during the campaign around Boston in 1775, the American War of Independence would have to be won by an army that could take on the British regulars in open battle. Some moves in this direction were made in June 1777, when George Washington's proposal that a standing army should be raised for the duration of the war was accepted by the Continental Congress, which authorized the creation of an army of 66,000 men to serve for the duration or three years.

Individual states were to raise a total of 83 battalions, which they would clothe and arm, while Congress would pay their officers and keep the army in the field. However, fewer than 15,000 men were raised. Morale sank when Washington's forces were defeated at the battles of the Brandywine, in September 1777, and Germantown a month later. The winter of 1777-78 was a miserable time for Washington's troops, who were based at Valley Forge. Some 3,000 men, most lacking warm clothing, equipment, food, and adequate shelter, were on the point of mutiny.

CONTINENTAL INFANTRY

However, morale improved early in 1778 when France agreed to a treaty with congress. At Valley Forge matters began to improve—discipline returned, desertion rates dropped, and the army slowly began to receive what it needed to take on the British. Many of these improvements were due to Baron Friedrich von Steuben, who instilled the necessary discipline in Washington's men. Steuben established set sizes for battalions (the average was around 250 men), and created a standardized drill program. Congress confirmed Steuben's plans in May 1778 by authorizing that battalions should consist of eight companies of 53 men and a light infantry company of similar strength.

The fruits of the French alliance, Washington's perseverance, and Steuben's practical reforms were seen at the Battle of Monmouth on June 28. Washington's men stood their ground and exchanged close-range volleys with the British. After the battle, which had lasted all day, the British were finally forced to retreat. However, the Continental Army was later beset by other problems—in January 1781, for example, some units mutinied, killing their officers. Grievances centered on the lack of pay and necessities.

It was not until October 1779 that Washington was able to issue specific dress regulations. Although there were always shortages of cloth, Continental infantry were supposed to wear blue coats, with different facings for groups of states. Remarkably, the army did not disintegrate and, because of Washington's will and the growing aid provided by the French, was able to inflict a decisive defeat on the British at the Battle of Yorktown in 1781, which effective guaranteed independence.

Washington's greatest achievement was to keep the Continental Army in being, despite all the problems he faced with regards to recruitment, pay, conditions, equipment, and training. That he did this in the middle of a war against a greatly superior enemy, one of the world's leading powers, ensured the preservation of the newly created nation.

FACT BOX

NATIONALITY **AMERICA**
LOCATION **COLONIAL AMERICA**

CAMPAIGNS
American War of Independence (1775-83)

TYPE: **INFANTRY**

77

FACTFINDER GUIDE: **WARRIORS**

Grenadier of the Imperial Guard

LATE 18TH AND EARLY 19TH CENTURY

NAPOLEAN'S GREANDIERS WERE DEFEATED AT WATERLOO.

The origins of Napoleon's Imperial Guard date back to the turmoil that followed the coup against the French Revolutionary government in 1799, which made Napoleon Bonaparte (1769-1821) the undisputed leader of France with the title of First Consul. Some of the troops who had supported the coup became known as the Guard of the Consuls on November 28, and would later be regarded as Napoleon's personal bodyguard and the most elite corps within his army.

From the outset, the Foot Grenadiers of the Guard was designed as an elite. Entry requirements were strict—the young and inexperienced were excluded and all successful recruits, mostly veterans, had to be over five feet six inches tall. Great emphasis was placed on drill, and the men received nearly double that of ordinary regiments. The Grenadiers were also given a uniform that would remain virtually unchanged throughout the Napoleonic Wars. This consisted a blue coat with white turn-backs, scarlet cuffs and epaulettes, and a large bearskin hat. White trousers with white gaiters completed the ceremonial uniform. On campaign, however, the uniform was simplified.

Napoleon's Imperial Guard, of which the Foot Grenadiers of the Guard were a part, was an all-arms force, consisting of artillery, cavalry, infantry, and various support services. The Imperial Guard varied in strength

78

GRENADIER OF THE IMPERIAL GUARD

throughout the Napoleonic Wars, but at its greatest, in 1812, it consisted of about 50,000 men. Of these, 14,000 were known as the Old Guard, of which the Foot Grenadiers were a part. Napoleon regarded this corps as his decisive reserve, one only to be unleashed to deliver the last blow against an enemy after his line units had inflicted sufficient damage. However, so successful were Napoleon's other troops that the Grenadiers, although present, did not play a direct part in many of his greatest victories. It seemed to many that Napoleon was unwilling to make full use of them on campaign.

Napoleon's desire to preserve the Imperial Guard is perhaps best shown during the hard-fought Battle of Borodino during his invasion of Russia in 1812. The emperor refused requests to order the Guard into the fray, stating: "I will not have my Guard destroyed 800 leagues from Paris." However, the subsequent retreat from Russia decimated the Imperial Guard, only 2,000 survived. In the campaigns of 1813-14 Napoleon was desperately short of troops and the Grenadiers were flung into several battles, fighting with great skill at, for example, Bautzen (May 1813), Dresden (August 1813), and Leipzig (October 1814). Napoleon was, however defeated and abdicated on April 11, 1814.

He was sent into exile with a personal bodyguard that included 300 Grenadiers, but returned to France in April 1815. His aim was to prevent the larger forces arrayed against him from linking up and to defeat them one by one. The Grenadiers led the final attack which crushed the Prussians at the Battle of Ligny on June 15, but the British escaped destruction at Quatre Bras on the same day. The decisive battle took place at Waterloo on the 18th. All day Napoleon launched attacks against the British, who were weakened but still fighting back. By around 7 pm, with the Prussians, who had been hurrying to Waterloo all day, seriously menacing Napoleon's right flank. Napoleon, believing the British were close to collapse unleashed his Foot Grenadiers. Blasted by artillery fire as they advanced in dense squares, the Grenadiers closed on the British line where, after heavy fighting, they were forced to retire. Napoleon's hopes of regaining his throne were swept away with his Grenadiers on the field of Waterloo.

FACT BOX

NATIONALITY	**FRENCH**
LOCATION	**EUROPE**

CAMPAIGNS
Napoleonic Wars

TYPE: **INFANTRY**

FACTFINDER GUIDE: **WARRIORS**

Wellington's Infantry

EARLY 19TH CENTURY

WELLINGTON'S INFANTRY HANDLED THE PRESSURES OF BATTLE WELL.

The British Army in the Napoleonic Wars never equaled the strength of those of the major continental European states, but regiment for regiment it was one of the best. Its great strength lay with its infantry, as the British cavalry arm was small and not always of the best quality. The weapons and training of the men who made up the infantry regiments were not dissimilar to their European counterparts, although the Brown Bess musket, accurate to around 120 yards, was considered a better weapon than most. However, the British infantry regiments were generally considered to be steadfast under fire.

The British were generally successful against the French not because their troops were significantly better, but because they evolved tactics that could successfully defeat the French, who had developed a fairly standardized battle plan. The French invariably attacked, unleashing their infantry in highly mobile but densely packed columns after an enemy had been softened up by massed artillery fire and weakened by aimed musketry from skirmishers. French cavalry would be used to charge unsteady infantry, attack any vulnerable flank, or pursue a routing foe.

Britain's Arthur Wellesley, the Duke of Wellington (1769-1852) developed the ideas that would defeat many French armies during the war in Spain against Napoleon. Wellington almost invariably took up strong defensive positions, often on high ground. His infantry were protected from enemy artillery fire by being sheltered behind the crest of the hill and only moved onto the crest when the French columns drew near. The French skirmishers were prevented from inflicting

WELLINGTON'S INFANTRY

damage on the British infantry because Wellington used skirmishers of his own who kept the French at a distance. Finally, he made sure that his flanks were protected, either by his own cavalry, the terrain, or fortifications.

French columns could move quickly but such a large mass made a tempting target for Wellington's own artillery, and few men in a French column could fire their own muskets, just those in the first few ranks or on the flanks. Against poorly disciplined or shaken infantry, however, the sight of a French column marching resolutely forward accompanied by drumbeats and cheers was enough to send them fleeing from the battlefield. Wellington's men were less impressed by the French columns, which they met in lines usually two ranks deep.

This meant that all the men in a British regiment could fire. At close range, the sustained fire of several British regiments could shatter a French column.

The British infantry also had a tactic to defeat French cavalry charges. The square, in which a regiment or regiments formed a four or three-sided formation that offered no open flanks, was not a British invention, but Wellington's troops proved particularly adept in its use. Infantry bayonets and volley fire prevented cavalry from getting into range to use their swords.

The value of Wellington's battlefield system was revealed at Waterloo in June 1815. Although his army, of which only part was British, was badly mauled, the tactics he developed in Spain allowed him to hold the French until his Prussian allies arrived to complete the defeat of Napoleon.

RIGHT: THE 88TH AT BADAJOZ IN 1812. FAR RIGHT: THE BATTLE OF WATERLOO.

FACT BOX

NATIONALITY **BRITISH**
LOCATION **WESTERN EUROPE**

CAMPAIGNS
Napoleonic Wars; the War of 1812

TYPE: **INFANTRY**

FACTFINDER GUIDE: **WARRIORS**

U.S. Infantry

EARLY 19TH CENTURY

GENERAL WINFIELD SCOTT AT THE BATTLE OF CHIPPEWA.

The war of 1812 (1812-15) was fought between the United States and Great Britain at the height of the Napoleonic Wars. The United States had become increasingly irritated by British warships stopping and searching US ships, and "hawks" in the US government began to agitate for an invasion of British-held Canada. On June 19, the United States declared war on Britain. Britain, however, had the much larger navy and its large army contained many battle-hardened regiments that had and were fighting the French in the Napoleonic Wars. In contrast, the total strength of the US Army in the month before the war began was just 6,000 men, although a program of rapid recruitment was instigated.

The men who enlisted went to war in a uniform not that different from the British in style. The wore a felt "shako," a short dark blue coat with red collar, and gaitered trousers in gray, green, or brown. However, the US, was short of suitable cloth and many regiments went to war in different uniforms. For example, the brigade commanded by General Winfield Scott, which fought with great distinction at the Battle of Chippewa (July 5, 1814), wore gray coats. The weapons carried by the troops varied but the main musket, produced in places such

82

U.S. INFANTRY

as Springfield and Harper's Ferry, was a copy of the 1777 French musket.

The tactics learned by the new recruits to the US Army had, through necessity, to be simple. Supported by artillery, infantry were supposed to advance in line to within 200 yards of the enemy before opening fire. As the distance closed to within 20 yards, the troops were ordered to shout, and then deliver a final volley at five yards before launching a bayonet charge. Throughout this, soldiers were taught to listen out for commands, load quickly, and aim low. These tactics were little different than those practiced by the British, but the British had used them in countless battles. Many US recruits had not seen action and some officers doubted that they could win a bayonet fight against British regulars.

The US Army was somewhat outclassed by the British during the opening battles on land, although they scored notable successes in several naval encounters on the Great Lakes, particularly the Battles of Lake Erie on September 10, 1813, and Lake Champlain, September 11, 1814. However, it was at Chippewa that the US Army's regulars came of age. Scott's brigade, some 1,400 men, were dressed in gray and the British commander believed them to be semi-trained militia. However, Scott's troops formed up with parade-ground precision while under fire and then advanced against the British line with fixed bayonets. The British fled the battlefield.

The victory won by Scott's brigade at Chippewa is commemorated at the United States Military Academy at West Point, which was officially founded in 1802. Trainee officers at the academy continue to wear gray uniforms. The war officially ended on December 24, 1814, but because of difficulties in transmitting the news, the last battle of the war was fought at New Orleans on January 8, 1815.

FACT BOX

NATIONALITY **AMERICAN**
LOCATION **NORTH AMERICAN**

CAMPAIGNS
The War of 1812

TYPE: **INFANTRY**

FACTFINDER GUIDE: **WARRIORS**

Union Soldier

MID-19TH CENTURY

The American Civil War, which broke out in 1861 and lasted until 1865, is regarded by many as the first modern war and in terms of men killed it was devastating. Of the nearly half a million fighting for the Confederate cause and over a million on the Unionist side, 622,000 lost their lives in often entrenched fighting. One reason for this is the first use of two modern weapons of destruction: the early machine gun and the repeating rifle.

At the outbreak of the war the United States Army was tiny, so volunteer and militia regiments had to be quickly raised and trained to fill the Unionist army. But after losses in the early years, particularly after the Battle of Gettysburg in June 1863, conscription was introduced in July 1863.

Because at first the Unionist army was made up of units assembled from many different sources and localities, the infantry carried a variety of weaponry. Although the more accurate rifle was preferred, shortages meant that many units carried outdated muskets and flintlocks instead. The standard US Army rifle at the outbreak of the war—the Minié—was widely used, but the most popular weapon was the US "Springfield" followed by the British Enfield — these were both rifles and had a longer range and were more accurate than older firearms. These weapons were generally muzzle-loading and had an attached bayonet but even when the combat was at close-quarters the latter was not often

UNION SOLDIER

used. The final weapon to be carried was a revolver. Usually this was a Colt, but the Remington and the British-made Deane and Adams were also used.

The uniform was generally a blue short jacket, with added unit insignia, and blue trousers plus knapsack, blanket, haversack (containing simple provisions), water bottle, and cartridge and cap boxes. The standard-issue headdress was a "képi." Officers wore a blue frock coat and broad-brimmed black felt hat, although many junior officers opted for the short jacket and képi.

The tactics of much of the warfare in the American Civil War generally favored defence and huge losses were suffered by both sides before the Unionists finally wore down the Confederates. Battles such as Gettysburg in 1863 presaged World War I in the heavy losses sustained by troops assaulting well-entrenched positions and huge frontal attacks in columns were gradually abandoned in favor of lines of skirmishers.

The war threw up some outstanding commanders on both sides, who quickly learned how to fight a modern war. The leading Unionist commander was General Ulysses S. Grant who was instrumental in the final victory of the northern states through such hard won victories as Vicksburg in 1863, which split the Confederacy in two, but he was ably assisted by such indomitable commanders as General W. T. Sherman, who led the final, all-consuming drive from Atlanta to finish off the war, and General P. H. Sheridan who laid the Shenandoah Valley to waste in 1864. Although at first the Unionist infantryman had been inexperienced, by the end of the war he was generally highly regarded for his discipline and bravery.

The Unionist cavalry, although unable to match the Confederates at the start of the war, was a match for its opponents by the end, and was arguably the most advanced cavalry in the world by the close of the war, having adapted to the first modern war. This plus the Unionist superiority in numbers, supplies and willpower led to the eventual victory of the North.

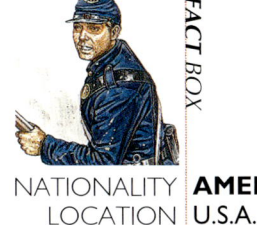

FAR LEFT: A PRIVATE IN THE 56TH US COLORED INFANTRY.

A UNION PRIVATE ON THE BATTLEFIELD.

FACT BOX

NATIONALITY	**AMERICAN**
LOCATION	U.S.A.

CAMPAIGNS
Various battles and campaigns of the American Civil War

TYPE: **INFANTRY**

85

FACTFINDER GUIDE: **WARRIORS**

Confederate Soldier

MID 19TH CENTURY

CONFEDERATE SOLDIERS WERE CONSIDERED SUPERIOR HORSEMEN.

Particularly at the start of the American Civil War, it was generally agreed that the Confederate states had the superior cavalry. The recruits were more dashing and generally better riders and their dress reflected this spirit, being slightly dandified. Western-type hats, which supplanted the képi-style hat inherited at the start of the war, were often adorned with feathers or plumes, hair was worn long, and jackets in standard Confederate gray with yellow collar and cuffs sported a wealth of braid. By the end of the war the lack of supplies and lack of discipline—troopers would often go missing during looting sprees—began to tell.

The American Civil War was one of the first wars of the 19th century where the advance of technology meant that the role of heavy cavalry was minimal in battle. Light horsemen, primarily armed with the short-barreled breech-loading carbine for ease of reloading, were vital, however, in scouting, screening, foraging, and deep raiding. These fighters were generally deployed at speed, dismounting to fight, making the saber redundant.

The weapons carried by the Confederate cavalryman were very similar to those borne by his Unionist counterpart: rifle or carbine, revolver, and saber. The muzzle-loading British Enfield was a popular carbine although on the Western front many Confederate cavalry preferred the more accurate longer barreled rifle or especially the Spencer magazine rifle.

Their most dashing commander was the cavalier General "Jeb" Stuart who commanded the Confederate Army of North Virginia. He excelled in gathering information on the opposing

86

CONFEDERATE SOLDIER

forces by operating far in advance of the main army and at times leading daring raids on enemy positions, although at one of the crucial battles of the war, Gettysburg in 1863, General Robert E. Lee, the great Confederate general, was crucially let down by Stuart's cavalry not keeping its position between the two armies. Instead, Stuart placed himself on the right flank of the enemy, severing communications with his commander who was unaware of the extent of the enemy advance and the strength of its position. The cavalry was subsequently also unable to help press home the Confederate attack, contributing to the defeat of Lee's army. Stuart was to die in battle in the next year trying to halt the advance of General Sheridan's Cavalry Corps of the Army of the Potomac toward the Confederate capital, Richmond, Virginia.

There were some notable cavalry victories, however, such as at Brice's Cross Roads, Mississippi in June 1864, where General Nathan Forrest, the famous commander of a Confederate cavalry division, defeated a much larger Unionist force in a brilliant attack.

The best of the Confederate infantry in the Army of Western Virginia under General Robert E. Lee was a match for the Unionists. Lee realized that the accuracy of the rifle meant that infantry tactics in battle had to change. Attacking forces could no longer advance in tightly grouped large formations and defensive field fortifications such as trenches, earthworks, and wire entanglements became increasingly important.

These lessons in attritional warfare were learnt the hard way after the Confederate army's defeat at the Battle of Shiloh in 1862 when their advance became one tangled group but by the time of the Battle of Cold Harbour in 1864 the Unionists suffered 13,000 casualties in one hour attacking well-defended Confederate lines, the defenders lost only 1,000. Subsequently, pioneered by General "Stonewall" Jackson, the value of covering fire during an attack was learned and the typical Confederate advance was conducted by successive lines in short rushes using available ground cover.

Heavily outnumbered throughout the war and often short of vital military supplies, the Confederate army fought with bravery and was led by commanding officers (eg. Lee and Jackson) of the highest quality.

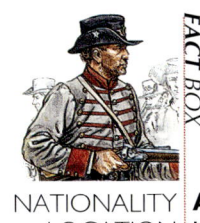

A PRIVATE IN THE 11TH MISSISSIPPI INFANTRY.

FACT BOX

NATIONALITY: **AMERICAN**
LOCATION: **U.S.A.**

CAMPAIGNS
Various battles and campaigns of the American Civil War

TYPE: **INFANTRY**

FACTFINDER GUIDE: **WARRIORS**

U.S. Cavalryman

LATE 19TH CENTURY

U.S. CAVALRY TROOPER, 1890S.

In the Indian Wars of 1866 to 1890, the US cavalryman was the spearhead of the United States' drive to impose its control on the plains of the Midwest and deserts of the Southwest of America, the last remaining heartlands of the Native American tribes. The frontier that needed to be patrolled was enormous and cavalry was the only effective force in these vast open spaces.

The ten cavalry regiments of the US Army were perhaps the best mounted troops in the world at the time. The four assigned to the frontier—the 7th to the 10th—forged a defiant, self-reliant, and professional ethos in these isolated conditions under the constant threat of attack and in the face of neglect by politicians.

The fighting was often unpleasant, both sides at times guilty of going beyond the normal rules of warfare, and life was generally hard. There was little training, the men being expected to learn the skills of horsemanship in the early months of their service, ammunition was often in short supply, the food was basic, and disease was a constant scourge. Drinking was about the only entertainment and discipline had to be harsh in these conditions. Many soldiers deserted before the final encounter at the Battle of Wounded Knee in 1890.

U.S. CAVALRYMAN

The US cavalryman was dressed typically in slouch hat or képi, bandanna, dark blue "sack coat" (officers coats had black braiding), which was a waist-length shell jacket, blue or gray shirt with yellow piping for officers, blue woollen trousers, long and heavy boots, and a caped overcoat during the winter. He was allowed a great deal of freedom in dress in the field, often appearing in civilian clothes and using civilian weapons.

He was typically armed with a Colt or Remington .44 cap-and-ball six-shooter revolver and a .50 caliber Springfield or 56/50 Spencer carbine. The saber was also occasionally carried by some officers.

The cavalry had two roles: as protection for encroaching US government control through escorting settlers or the mail and protecting the building of railways, etc., as well as actively pursuing the war against hostile Native American tribes. The latter often took the form of scouting parties to track bands of marauding braves. Often these cavalry scouting parties would attempt to keep the nuisance of attacks down by putting the bands of braves on the defensive so that large-scale battles were avoided. Long-distances were covered in the campaigns as the enemy was gradually worn down, often in winter when it was harder for the braves to live off the land, so the cavalry took its own wagon train of supplies with it on these expeditions.

Famous US Cavalry names include Major-General Philip H. Sheridan, who masterminded many of the campaigns of the Indian Wars where the policy was to destroy Native American villages and horse herds. The intention was to drive the marauding braves out of the territory and onto reservations.

Another important figure was Brigadier-General Alfred H. Terry who led the cavalry in the wars against the plains Native Americans in the 1870s. However, the most famous name is Lieutenant-Colonel George A. Custer of the 7th Cavalry Regiment who led the attack on the Cheyenne village of Washita in 1868 taking his forces to destruction and meeting his own end at the Battle of Little Big Horn, Montana, in 1876, against a combined Sioux and Cheyenne force led by Sitting Bull and Crazy Horse.

FACT BOX

NATIONALITY **AMERICAN**
LOCATION **U.S.A.**

CAMPAIGNS
Various battles and campaigns of the Indian Wars

TYPE: **CAVALRY**

FACTFINDER GUIDE: **WARRIORS**

Apache Brave

LATE 19TH CENTURY

THE APACHE BRAVE ROAMED THE DESERTS OF THE SOUTHWESTERN U.S.

The Native American brave was arguably the finest light cavalryman of the age. Able to operate in often harsh environments, having enormous stamina, and being a master of concealment and ambush, he could usually outdistance the heavy US Cavalry horse on his lighter pony.

The Apache warrior was particularly renowned as a warlike raider and fierce marauder in the territory of the deserts of southwestern United States. These fighters had grown up used to athletic pursuits—learning to value bravery, to fight and to endure pain as part of their culture. In addition, the Apaches lived in small semi-nomadic bands to avoid being surprised by enemy attack as they were often at odds with other Apache bands. When raiding, their main aim was not to kill, but they would go to war to revenge deaths and were responsible for as many acts of cruelty as their enemies.

Fighting tactics were hit and run, by day and night, sniping and ambushing using gunfire or arrows. The direct frontal attack was not their

APACHE BRAVE

style of warfare; they preferred instead circling attacks or ambushes.

The traditional Apache warrior's garb was a kilt, breech-clout and buckskin leggings, moccasins, and turbaned headdress although they often fought semi-naked. Their weapons were a lance, a war club—a stone head wrapped in buckskin on a wooden handle—and a wooden bow stringed with sinew. Arrows were long and finished with steel tips that would often detach themselves in the body of the enemy. Usually a rawhide shield was also carried.

In addition, the Apache brave was often armed with guns—albeit outmoded—from the Indian Bureau. These could be muzzle-loading rifles such as the Lancaster, the Hawken percussion rifle, or an early Springfield, muskets, or a percussion gun with either half or full stock. Even flintlocks were used when percussion caps were not readily available. As good horsemen they could fire these weapons while slipped to the side of the horse to protect themselves from returned gunfire.

Even before the Indian Wars of the second half of the 19th century the Apache had developed a reputation for aggression when fighting against other Native American tribes in the area as well as against Spanish invaders and the Mexicans. These conflicts demonstrated the skills of the great Apache leaders, first Cochise and then Geronimo and Naiche. The chiefs would personally lead their braves but they were adept at avoiding full-scale battles with the US Cavalry so that the Apaches were only fully subjugated onto reservations after Geronimo finally surrendered in 1886, being worn down by living on the run in the mountains for so long.

For years they lived off the land and harried the US army, attacking silently and then disappearing into the wilderness. A measure of their quality as pioneering guerrilla fighters is that for a remarkable 25 years these tactics helped prolong their campaign against the vastly superior firepower and artillery of the US Army.

FACT BOX

NATIONALITY NATIVE AMERICAN
LOCATION U.S.A.

CAMPAIGNS
Various battles and campaigns of the Indian Wars

TYPE: LIGHT CAVALRY

FACTFINDER GUIDE: **WARRIORS**

Zulu Impi Warrior

LATE 19TH CENTURY

THE ZULUS DEALT THE ENGLISH ONE OF THE MOST SERIOUS DEFEATS OF THEIR COLONIAL WARS.

The Zulu nation, formed in the early 19th century, soon created a reputation amongst its neighbors as a fearsome fighting force under King Shaka. The Zulu War of 1879, under the new king Cetshwayo, against the British was, however, to be last great conflict of this warrior nation.

The main Zulu army at the time comprised a formidable 20,000 warriors and was commanded by Chiefs Mnyamana and Ntshingwayo. Other respected military leaders were Chiefs Zibhebu and Sigcwelegcwele and Prince Dabulamanzi. In the Zulu nation, once a young man reached 18 or 19 he was called up and placed in a regiment with his contemporaries, under the king's "izinduna" (officers). He remained in the king's service until his thirties, forging a powerful esprit de corps with his comrades, before he was allowed to marry, passing to the national reserve list.

The Zulu warrior's wardress was made up of feathers and furs denoting the regiment but most went into battle wearing little more than loin-coverings. A large, oval, hide shield with regimental markings, a 12-18 inch-long stabbing spear ("assegai"), and, occasionally, a lighter throwing spear or club ("knobkerry") were carried. Firearms were also widespread but these were generally obsolete types (although a significant amount were captured in victories early in the war against the British, but ammunition was in short supply and the warriors were generally untrained in their use).

Tactics generally were to fight at close quarters, knocking the opponent off-balance with the shield before thrusting with the spear. The custom was to disembowl a dead enemy and wear items of his clothing until cleansing ceremonies had taken place. This could be counter-productive though—after their great victory at Isandlwana these rituals meant that the Zulus were unable to follow up their gains because the army had dispersed to perform the cleansing ceremonies.

One of the strengths of the Zulu army in the difficult terrain in which the war was fought was its mobility in comparison to the British Army, which

92

ZULU IMPI WARRIOR

required large-scale back-up in supplies. The typical attack by a Zulu armed force ("impi") was nicknamed the "beast's horns," and consisted of a frontal assault ("the chest") by senior regiments with encircling movements on both sides ("the horns") by the junior regiments to surround the enemy. This could be achieved at great speed as at the first major conflict of the Zulu War when the main Zulu impi overran the British 24th Regiment's camp at Isandlwana.

In spite of the British firepower, which included two seven-pounder guns, the 24th was caught before it could form a tight defensive group. This was the worst defeat suffered by the British Army in all its colonial wars: the 1,700-strong camp was virtually entirely wiped out, although the Zulus also suffered heavy losses in the attack, with over 1,000 killed.

The ultimate failure of the Zulu army to overcome the firepower of a European army was shown by the next famous encounter of the war: the Battle of Rorke's Drift. Here, the 4,000-strong Undi corps under Prince Dabulamanzi failed in over 12 hours of continual attack to overcome just over 100 British soldiers defending a mission station. After this, Cetshwayo wanted to avoid attacking well-defended positions, planning to lure the British into the open instead, but over-confidence among the Zulu warriors in their ability to overcome any British force if they attacked in large enough numbers led to their downfall at the decisive battle of the war—Khambula. At Khambula the British were prepared and with just over 2,000 men, four seven-pounders, and two unattached guns routed a Zulu force of over 20,000 warriors.

Ultimately, the Zulus failed because although they came from a well-organized military culture, obedience to overall strategy was not always strong. Both Isandlwana and Khambula took place against the wishes of the Zulu leaders and at Khambula the over-eagerness of the right horn meant that the Zulu attack was fragmented. Crucially, they also underestimated the devastating firepower of the British Army's Martini-Henry rifle and found it hard to break down well-organized defences, meeting their destruction in the hail of fire before they could engage at close quarters.

FACT BOX

NATIONALITY **ZULU, PART OF TODAY'S SOUTH AFRICA**

LOCATION SOUTHERN AFRICA

CAMPAIGNS
1879 Zulu War, including Battles of Isandlwana, Rorke's Drift, Khambula and Ulundi

TYPE: **WARRIORS**

FACTFINDER GUIDE: **WARRIORS**

Boer Sharpshooter

LATE 19TH CENTURY–EARLY 20TH CENTURY

TWO BOER COMMANDERS PICTURED IN 1901.

In the Boer War of 1899-1902 the Boers took on the British Army, which was regarded as the most powerful army in the world at the time, and taught it a harsh lesson. The Boer armed forces had been honed after years of defending first their territory in the Cape against the Xhosa, then their republics of Orange Free State and Transvaal against the Zulus and the British. In fact, they had already inflicted defeats on the British Army in the first Boer War of 1880-1.

Although not a professional army and despite the occasional lack of discipline in the field by these part-time solders, the Boers were a match for anyone. They were at home in the hot climate, well-armed with modern firearms, superb marksmen even when mounted, and well versed in fieldcraft and fighting from concealed entrenchments wearing camouflaged clothing. Uniforms were generally self-provided although the slouch hat, which gave protection from the sun, was generally worn.

Having grown up hunting on the veld, the typical Boer had developed accurate marksmanship and the art of concealment from an early age. This influenced their tactics, which were to hold the enemy front with skirmishers while using cover to gallop round to the flanks, dismounting and advancing on the enemy with overwhelming fire. They were ably supported by excellent field artillery manufactured by Krupps, and four Schneider siege guns. The sharpshooters were the mainstay of the Boer army. These snipers used smokeless powder which made it impossible to detect their position. Under the Boer commander, De La Rey, the devastating effect of the riflemen was soon realized, being first deployed at low-level at the famous Battle of Magersfontein.

The British-made Martini-Henry rifle was originally widely used by the Boers, but being a single-shot weapon was superseded by the Mauser. The Mauser magazine rifle, capable of great accuracy, was far superior to the Lee-Enfield MKII and Lee-Metford rifles used by the British. It had a greater range—with glasses it could be targeted up to 3,000 yards—and the British often found themselves pinned down in the field by this weapon.

After the Boer capital of Pretoria was lost to the British, the war was prolonged for two years, principally through the actions of the skilled guerilla fighters Generals Christiaan de Wet and Jan Smuts in highly mobile Commando units. The word "commando" means self-contained Boer raiding column. These were small groups, each derived from a specific district, which were mobile and generally mounted. They made the most of their knowledge of the terrain to attack British posts, sabotage railway lines, and tie up large numbers of troops. They were only defeated when Kitchener, in overall command of the British Army at this stage of the war, blocked the Commandos supply lines to the local farms through the use of blockades and his controversial concentration camps of civilians sympathetic to the Boer forces.

The Boers were adept at defence as well as attack. In an advance warning of the changing nature of warfare, as firepower had become so powerful, their well-sited and expertly concealed trenches and their use of barbed wire were able to hold off superior British forces, especially in the early battles of the war at Magersfontein and Modder River under General De La Rey, and Colenso under Louis Botha. However, the number of long and unsuccessful sieges in the Boer War—most famously, Mafeking, Ladysmith, and Kimberley—shows up a weakness in Boer tactics. Used to waiting for the enemy to surrender, they were to lose the initiative in this war when the British managed to hold out long enough to reinforce their army and eventually make their superiority in numbers tell in the defeat of the Boers in open warfare.

FACT BOX

NATIONALITY | **BOER–AFRIKANER PEOPLES OF SOUTH AFRICA**
LOCATION | SOUTH AFRICA, CENTERED ON THE BOER REPUBLICS OF TRNSVAAL AND ORANGE FREE STATE

CAMPAIGNS
Boer War, including the sieges of Ladysmith, Kimberley and Mafeking 1899-1900; Battles of Stormberg 1899, Modder River, Magersfontein 1899, Colenso 1899, Spion Kop 1900, Paardeberg 1900, Moderspruit and Pretoria 1900, Berg-en dal 1900

TYPE: **SHARPSHOOTER**

FACTFINDER GUIDE: **WARRIORS**

World War I

A FRENCH COUPLE, IMPRISONED UNDER GERMAN RULE, THANK THEIR AMERICAN LIBERATORS AT THE END OF WORLD WAR I.

WORLD WAR I

FACTFINDER GUIDE: **WARRIORS**

German Stormtrooper

STORMTROOPERS WITH FLAMETHROWERS AND HAND GRENADES.

The elite infantry of the German Army, the "Stosstruppen" or Stormtroops, nearly won World War I for Germany. Born in 1915 out of the deadlock on the Western Front, the Stormtroops developed modern infantry tactics.

In contrast to the conventional large blocs of infantry in static skirmish lines armed only with the magazine-loading rifle, the German Stormtroops were organized in highly mobile small units and armed with a range of weaponry: the eight-round Luger pistol, light machine guns, the MG "08/15" or often captured British Lewis guns, mortars, grenade launchers, stick and egg hand grenades, and flamethrowers.

The K.98 carbine was adopted because it was shorter and lighter than the standard-issue Mauser and, in the short combat range of trench warfare, no less accurate; the MP18 sub-machine gun was also highly effective at close quarters, and small field guns were often brought into battle.

One item of uniform was the distinctively shaped "Stahlhelm." Covering the ears and the back of the neck this was to become an instantly recognisable feature of the German soldier in later years, although at the time it was not widespread amongst the regular German Army. Ankle boots and puttees were preferred to the standard jackboots for ease of movement.

Originally formed as an experimental battalion in 1915, the dynamic leadership of Captain Willy Ernst Rohr persuaded General Ludendorff that Stormtroop battalions should be created throughout the German army and the attack on Verdun in February 1916 was led by Stormtroop detachments.

GERMAN STORMTROOPER

In time, the Stormtroops were organized into battalions subdivided into machine gun companies, flamethrower platoons, infantry gun batteries, mortar companies etc, co-ordinating their attacks and maximizing firepower and movement.

They were used to spearhead German attacks or for rapid and violent counter-attack. Able to overwhelm entrenched defences, they punched holes through enemy lines and advanced at a rate that was astonishing. The last desperate German attempt to win the war in March 1918 saw the culmination of the development of Stormtrooper tactics. In order to advance quickly, stubborn enemy positions were bypassed and heavy weapons had to be brought by hand with the forward troops. In the end, however, the death-toll of the best German troops was too high and the offensive failed.

The Stormtroopers were drawn from fit, battle-hardened soldiers. Individual initiative was encouraged and unlike other more class-bound armies of the time, NCOs provided valuable tactical leadership. Their status as elite shock attack troops was reflected in the better rations they received than the regular troops; they were also kept at the front for shorter periods to keep them fresh.

Training for specific battle topographies was important, the success of this was demonstrated by the closely related German Mountain Corps, which had acclimatized to operate effectively in the mountains before the Battle of Caporetto in October 1917 in the Alps which destroyed the Italian Army.

Despite being the most effective infantry force of the war, the Stormtroops could not win the war for Germany. The inability of the rest of the German Army to support them fast enough and in enough depth meant that the superior resources of the Allies were to finally tell.

FACT BOX

NATIONALITY **GERMAN**
LOCATION WESTERN FRONT (BELGIUM AND FRANCE) 1915-18, ITALY 1917-18.

CAMPAIGNS
Western Front: Battle of Verdun 1916, Battle of the Somme 1916, Battle of Ypres 1917, Battle of Passchendaele 1917, Aisne Offensive, 1917, Battle of Cambrai 1917, German Spring 1918 Offensive, Allied Summer-Autumn 1918 Counter-Offensive;
Italy: Battle of Caporetto 1917

TYPE: **INFANTRY**

FACTFINDER GUIDE: **WARRIORS**

French Poilu

FRENCH TROOPS NEAR HOUTHEN IN 1917.

The French Army of World War I suffered huge losses in the defence of its homeland. From the start it was the French Army which bore the brunt of the German "Blitzkrieg" in August 1914, preventing them from reaching the Channel ports and Paris in an attempt to finish the war early, and turning them back at the Battle of the Marne, September 1914.

The French Army of the time was, however, instilled with the cult of attack being the best form of defence and in turn planned to invade Germany by taking Alsace and Lorraine. Full of vigor and the will to succeed, speed was regarded as the essence of modern combat and the bayonet was the chosen weapon. This bold offensive, however, planned by French commander General Joffre, resulted in heavy French losses and became bogged down in stalemate.

Joffre realized that tactics would have to change and that the French Army would have to make a huge sacrifice to save the country, replenishing itself through conscription, and accepting heavy losses as the price of the war. By the end of the war France was to have lost an estimated 1.4 million men through this strategy of a war of attrition, which by then was being continued by General Foch.

France was one of the few major powers to start the war with its soldiers not in camouflaged uniforms but in the traditional blue jacket and red

FRENCH POILU

trousers. Even at the end of the war the standard field uniform was blue. Nevertheless, the high casualty rate of World War I due to the huge amount of high explosive and shrapnel head injuries led to many developments in equipment and uniform. To protect the head, the French Army pioneered the modern military helmet, known as the "casque Adrian," by the end of 1915 for the regular French soldier.

The standard infantry weapon for the "poilu" (nickname for private) was the 8mm "Lebel" M.1886/93 rifle (although this was superseded by the Berthier 07/15) and bayonet. A variety of grenades were also carried. Officers carried an 8mm Lebel revolver. Cavalry regiments were armed with 8mm carbines, sabers, and even occasionally lances. Specialist units also were armed with the Hotchkiss model 1914 machine gun, or 8mm light machine gun.

The most famous campaign of World War I for the French was the Battle of Verdun. This was the longest battle of the war, lasting from February to December 1916, and came to symbolize French resistance and national willpower. The fortified city of Verdun was the scene of an enormous German infantry and artillery attack that was intended to bleed dry the French army. The battle zone came to resemble another world, but among the craters the French defenders held off repeated German attacks with their own massive artillery bombardments. Final casualties on both sides totaled nearly a million.

Their courage and ability to persevere in spite of the appalling conditions, horrific sights, fear, as well as continual bombardment are a testament to the endurance of the French poilu, fighting to defend his country. These qualities allied to the ability of France to maintain its industrial output during the war, sustaining its army with armaments and supplies, despite being partially occupied, were vital to holding back the Germans until the Allies' forces could enforce victory.

FACT BOX

NATIONALITY **FRENCH**
LOCATION **WESTERN FRONT: FRANCE AND BELGIUM**

CAMPAIGNS
Western Front: Battle of the Marne 1914, Battle of Verdun 1916, Battle of the Somme 1916, Battles of Ypres 1914, 1915, 1917, Battle of Passchendaele 1917, Aisne Offensive 1917, Battle of Cambrai 1917, German Spring 1918 Offensive, Allied Summer-Autumn 1918 Counter-Offensive

TYPE: **INFANTRY**

FACTFINDER GUIDE: **WARRIORS**

British Tommy

BRITISH TROOPS WAIT IN A SUPPORT TRENCH.

Unlike the other great Western powers involved at the start of World War I, the British Army was professional. This well trained and well prepared army was arguably the most efficient fighting force of the war but it was small (a quarter of a million soldiers). The British Expeditionary Force under Field Marshal Sir John French was dispatched to France in August 1914 and despite a reluctance on the part of its commanders to engage the advancing German army and possibly lose the entire force, kept its coherence and *ésprit de corps* during what was in effect continuous retreat.

At the Battle of Mons in August 1914, it delayed the Germans just enough through the extremely high rate of its disciplined and accurate rifle and artillery fire to help the French stop the Blitzkrieg at the Battle of the Marne.

Under the organization of Lord Kitchener, a mass army was built from first volunteers then conscription from 1916. Sir Douglas Haig replaced French in 1915 as he was better prepared for the long attritional struggle. This new army brought in people with no military background yet who felt the urge to serve their country. Many battalions were formed from close-knit groups and these became known as "Pals" battalions. This camaraderie helped them survive the grim trench warfare but the heavy losses meant whole communities were decimated. By the end of the war Britain also drew heavily on other countries throughout its Empire, such as Canada, India, and Australia, for additional troops.

BRITISH TOMMY

The British service uniform was khaki and standard issue weapons were Mills bomb grenades and the famously reliable .303 SMLE (Short Magazine Lee-Enfield) Mark III rifle plus bayonet. Officers carried the Webley revolver. Later, a gas mask was also carried. However, it took until 1916 for the army to be fully equipped with steel helmets.

Specialist weapons included mortars, the Vickers machine gun, and Lewis light machine gun. The developing technology of war and the nature of the fighting in the trenches meant the standard infantry attack also changed into using single files of men equipped with the range of this specialist weaponry.

The changing nature of modern warfare was traumatically brought home to this new army at the Battle of the Somme in July 1916 when it suffered over 57,000 casualties in the first day of what was intended to be the big push to end the war. By November, when the positions of the opposing forces had not markedly changed, the British Army had suffered 420,000 casualties in the offensive.

Although this new army was not as highly trained as the original British Expeditionary Force it was an effective fighting force with good morale, supported by heavy artillery that gradually became more targeted. Using brief but fierce hurricane bombardments and the effective creeping bombardment just ahead of the attacking troops to keep the enemy quiet, artillery was crucial to an attack. Having survived the desperate German offensive in the spring of 1918, the British Army was finally able to co-ordinate a series of large-scale attacks, advancing at speed for the first time in the war. This "Hundred Days Battle" was to break the German Army, which by fall of that year was ready to sue for peace.

FACT BOX

NATIONALITY	BRITISH AND OTHER COUNTRIES IN THE EMPIRE, INCLUDING INDIA, CANADA, AUSTRALIA AND NEW ZEALAND.
LOCATION	WESTERN FRONT: FRANCE, and BELGIUM.

CAMPAIGNS
Western Front: Battle of the Marne 1914, Battle of Verdun 1916, Battle of the Somme 1916, Battles of Ypres 1914, 1915, 1917, Battle of Passchendaele 1917, Aisne Offensive 1917, Battle of Cambrai 1917, German Spring 1918 Offensive, Allied Summer-Autumn 1918 counter-offensive. Other campaigns: Gallipoli 1915, Palestine 1917-18, East Africa 1914-18, Italy 1917-18

TYPE: **INFANTRY**

FACTFINDER GUIDE: **WARRIORS**

U.S. Doughboy

US "DOUGHBOYS" CROSS INTO GERMAN TERRITORY.

The US did not enter World War I until 1917 but the influx of fresh new troops from the US in the field in 1918, the "Doughboys" as they were nicknamed, was vital in the Allies' final victory against Germany in 1918.

In command of the American Expeditionary Force (AEF) was General John J. Pershing who successfully resisted British and French attempts to take command and use the army only to plug holes amongst their own troops. Initially, this army was small, badly equipped, and by no means ready to go into combat, but by the end of the war it was to number nearly two million soldiers, comprised of volunteers and drafted men. The numbers grew rapidly from about 160,000 at the front in March, to a million in September and double that again by November.

The amount of front line held by the Americans—they had the southerly part—also grew at the same rate. In the crucial battles of September 1918 the Americans played an important part in the breaking of the German Army in the battles of Belleau Woods and Chateau-Thierry.

104

U.S. DOUGHBOY

At the German salient of St Mihiel 500,000 US troops with 174 tanks under Colonel Patton pushed back the enemy, capturing 15,000 prisoners. Later in September, the US were able to contribute 189 tanks, 800 aircraft, and nine divisions to the Meuse-Argonne offensives.

Because the US entered the war late, its soldiers had to catch up on the expertise of trench warfare that the other armies had gained. Its characteristics were dash, energy, and confidence but this enthusiasm led to heavy casualties (over 300,000 in less than one year) in spite of Pershing's refusal to commit his army in combat until he felt it was ready.

Inexperience meant that their courage and enthusiasm led them to make frontal attacks on well-protected and undamaged German lines, often outpacing their own supply lines in the process. Many famous names, however, emerged from the US Army in World War I such as Douglas MacArthur, George Marshall, and George Patton.

Although at first the Americans often relied on British and French supplies, they developed their army as a separate force. The uniform was olive drab with a British-style steel helmet and the personal weapon was the Springfield rifle. Specialist infantry weaponry also included the Hotchkiss light machine gun.

By the end of the war the American ability to organize the logistics of their army effectively was in evidence. The Army had been split in two, comprising the American First and Second Armies. This reorganization allowed the Armies to advance faster as lines of command were more manageable.

Also, by this time the industrial support from the American economic powerhouse was beginning to work at full capacity, ensuing a steady flow of vital heavy artillery, tanks, aircraft, etc. In the end, the psychological impact of the arrival of the Americans was crucial, giving fresh heart to the Allies and making the Germans feel they were fighting a losing battle in terms of men and armaments.

FACT BOX

NATIONALITY **AMERICAN**
LOCATION **WESTERN FRONT: FRANCE AND BELGIUM**

CAMPAIGNS
German Spring 1918 Offensive, Allied Summer-Autumn 1918 counter-offensive: Cantigny, Chateau Thierry, Belleau Wood, Second Battle of the Marne, St Mihiel, Meuse-Argonne Offensive

TYPE: **INFANTRY**

FACTFINDER GUIDE: **WARRIORS**

German Airman

GERMAN SOLDIERS AND THE ALBATROSS DIII FIGHTER PLANE.

Although the first manned flight took place only just over 10 years before the outbreak of World War I, the war in the air was vital to each of the armies involved. It took place close to the ground war: airfields were only a few miles behind the front and combat was usually only a few thousand feet above the trenches. Verdun, for instance, saw particularly intensive fighting in the air, mirroring the carnage on the ground.

Although the German Flying Corps was initially employed for reconnaissance, ensuring army artillery was ranged correctly, destroying enemy observation balloons, and supporting campaigns on the ground; the air aces of the German Flying Corps were often engaged in deadly dogfights against enemy scouts to control the airspace as well as being vulnerable to attack from the ground. Even the unreliable machines themselves could be a hazard.

The rate of progress in military aviation during the war was astonishing. At the start of the war, pilots and observers were equipped only with rifles and pistols; in 1915 the Fokker E1 monoplanes were fitted with interrupter gear, allowing a machine gun to fire along the line of flight through the propeller arc without damaging the propeller blades. These Fokker monoplanes ruled the skies in 1915, being superior to Allied aircraft in maximum speed and altitude and able to dive almost vertically. Famous pilots such

GERMAN AIRMAN

as Werner Voss, Max Immelman (who developed the famous "Immelman" turn: a half loop and roll to get above an enemy attacking from the rear), Oswald Boelcke, and Baron Von Richthofen, nicknamed the "Red Baron" on account of painting his aircraft red, and who shot down a record 80 enemy aircraft before his death in 1918, developed new tactics which included the use of fighter planes escorting the scouts for the first time. In time these would develop into large fighting formations.

In 1916, the German Flying Corps organized its best pilots into squadrons to use the new Albatros DIII fighter which was sturdier, faster, and more maneuverable than the Allied aircraft. It had a ceiling of 18,000 feet, a top speed of 110 mph, fired two Spandau machine guns through the propeller, and was able to strafe ground troops. This was followed by the even more advanced D-type fighters as the Germans again seized the initiative in the race for superiority. The most famous of these was the outstanding Fokker DVII single-seat biplane which appeared in 1918: easy to fly, it had good visibility, was uniquely maneuverable, and well armed with two synchronized Spandau machine guns.

The Germans also developed bombers during the war and the Zeppelin raids on England should not be forgotten, but these had no serious impact on the war. Although at times dominating the skies, the German Flying Corps, like its counterpart on the ground, lost the war in spite of late advances such as the all-metal Junkers D1 single-seat fighter, the CLI two-seat fighter/ground attack aircraft and the 180 mph single-seat fighter-scout Pfalz DXII, by being overwhelmed by ultimately superior forces.

FACT BOX

NATIONALITY **GERMAN**
LOCATION **PRIMARILY THE WEST FRONT: FRANCE AND BELGIUM.**

CAMPAIGNS
Mons 1914, Le Cateau 1914, The Marne 1914/1918, Neuve Chapelle 1915, Artois 1915, Loos 1915, Verdun 1916, The Somme 1916, Ypres 1914/1915/1917, Passchandaele 1917, Arras 1917, Aisne 1917, Cambrai 1917, German Spring 1918 Offensive, Allied Summer-Autumn 1918 Counter-Offensive, Amiens 1918, Argonne Forest 1918

TYPE: **AIR FORCE**

FACTFINDER GUIDE: **WARRIORS**

Royal Flying Corps Airman

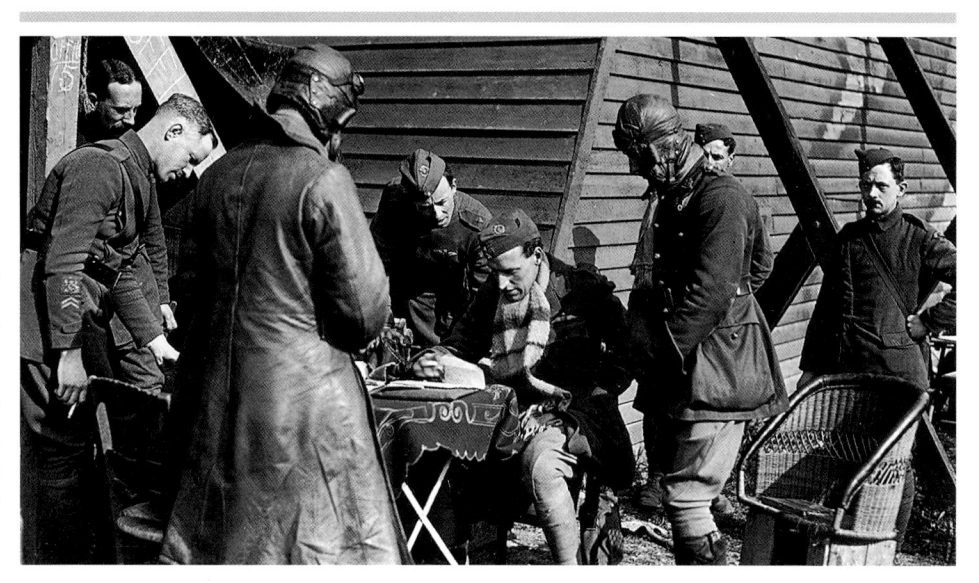

PILOTS REPORT BACK TO THEIR COMMANDER.

The start of World War I saw the Royal Flying Corps, recently formed in 1912, take a small armada of primitive flying machines across the Channel. Despite the appallingly high casualty rates (parachutes were not carried and aircrew could even occasionally be pitched out of the aircraft during violent maneuvers), by November 1918 the Royal Air Force, formed April 1, 1918 and incorporating the RFC, numbered nearly 300,000 men and 22,000 aircraft. It had played a crucial part in the Allied victory, taking over the reconnaissance role from the cavalry which had been unable to move freely in the trench warfare and using photography and wireless communications.

The airmen flew open to the elements and despite wearing as many layers as possible, including fur-lined outer garments with leather gauntlets, flying mask and thigh boots, cold was a great enemy at altitude, especially in winter, so much so that airmen frequently suffered from frostbite. In 1916, the first flying suit, the "Sidcot," was developed which protected the airman from the worst of the cold.

The recruits were picked to be fearless: young—mostly in their late teens or early twenties—fit, alert, happy-go-lucky, and generally unmarried, they were inexperienced, and training was brief. Initially, there were no tactics but these early reconnaissance aircraft soon ran into enemy aircraft intent on the same mission and air combat was born. New recruits with only a few hours flying time under their belts had no time to learn to survive in the air and were lost at a very high rate. Ground fire, early anti-aircraft fire from shelling as well as rifles, was also

108

ROYAL FLYING CORPS AIRMAN

a danger to the aircraft, which at first could only reach an altitude of a few thousand feet.

By 1915, RFC aircraft were fitted with the Vickers or lighter Lewis machine guns, although it was some time before they were fitted with interrupter gear enabling them to fire through the propeller arc. Tracer fire was first used by the RFC in 1916 at the Somme, allowing the gunner to see if his line of fire was accurate. In time, tactics developed and squadrons consisting of larger numbers of fighter aircraft protected each other in the air, flying in tight V-formation and attacking in pairs. Bombing against enemy troops and supply lines, often in the dark and particularly targeting railways, developed also.

Although at the start of the war RFC aircraft were inferior to those of the Germans, intensive development meant that eventually British aircraft such as the Bristol F2A fighter-scout biplane, introduced in 1917, and the highly maneuverable Sopwith Camel and SE5, could take on the Germans. RFC aces such as Edward Mannock, Albert Ball, Billy Bishop, and James McCudden matched the famous German names.

Under its commander, Hugh Trenchard, the RFC fought a war of aggression against the German Air Force. The philosophy was similar to that of the ground battle: to defeat the enemy through a war of attrition, accepting high losses. Although many paid a high price, the RFC ultimately managed to control the airspace above the battlefield, assisting the Allied Army in its final victory.

TOP: CAPTAIN ALBERT BALL.   BELOW: OFFICERS NEAR YPRES.

FACT BOX

NATIONALITY **BRITISH AND OTHER COUNTRIES FROM THE EMPIRE.**

LOCATION **PRIMARILY THE WESTERN FRONT: FRANCE AND BELGIUM**

CAMPAIGNS
Mons 1914, Le Cateau 1914, The Marne 1914/1918, Neuve Chapelle, Loos 1915, The Somme 1916, Ypres 1914/1915/1917, Passchandaele 1917, Arras 1917, Aisne 1917, Cambrai 1917, Spring 1918 Offensive, Amiens 1918, Hindenburg Line 1918

TYPE: **AIR FORCE**

FACTFINDER GUIDE: **WARRIORS**

British Tank Crew

INSPECTING A GERMAN ANTI-TANK RIFE.

The British led in the development of the tank, which first appeared on the Somme battlefield in 1916. The Tank Corps, formed in 1917, recognized the potential of the tank as a decisive weapon to provide close support for infantry. Intended to resist machine gun fire and overcome barbed wire, mud and shell holes with the weight of its distinctive lozenge-shaped body spread on caterpiller tracks, the early machines were armed with two six-pounder cannon or four side-mounted Vickers machine guns on "sponsons" (half-turrets) plus a Hotchkiss machine gun. The main battle tank was the MkI, which was developed throughout the war, reaching the MkV model, but in spring 1918 the faster Medium A Whippet was also introduced, although this was more of an armored car on tracks, armed only with machine guns.

At first the tank was used piecemeal and the lumbering vehicles became bogged down in the trenches, prone to mechanical breakdown or German shelling, due to their weak armor plating and top speed of under five mph. However, the potential to break the deadlock of trench warfare could be seen when enough tanks could be put in the field as at Cambrai in 1917 where 378 took part in the first tank battle, and Amiens in 1918 where 534 were used in an attack. At Cambrai, the tanks attacked with no preliminary bombardment and the

BRITISH TANK CREW

element of surprise was vital, but even at these two battles the losses were extremely high—only six tanks were still operable by the fourth day of Amiens. In addition, infantry support, particularly at Cambrai, was slow and the breakthrough could not be supported in spite of the initially relatively low British losses compared to the Germans.

The tanks carried a crew of eight: commander, driver, four gunners, and two gearsmen to steer the vehicle. In the cramped interior, battle conditions were harsh for the crew, being noisy, hot, and full of choking fumes from the uncovered engine. The crew and the tank's contents would be thrown about as the machine lurched along and communications between the crew had to be made by hand signals because of the noise. As an untried new weapon, training was sketchy and commanders were given little assistance in navigation. Once a tank lost its way and was halted the crew had to fight on in what could be a death trap although crew-members were only lightly armed with a pistol, generally the .455 Webley revolver. At Passchendaele, one crew fought off German troops for three days after their tank got bogged down in the mud.

The tank was a new weapon and it took a while for the army to make best use of it. Although the machines terrified the enemy and could break through lines with minimal losses of men, it was not until the last few months of the war that they were effectively used to spearhead attacks with infantry in close support.

TOP: BRITISH MARK V TANKS IN MEAULTE. INSET: A WHIPPET TANK.

FACT BOX

NATIONALITY	**BRITISH**
LOCATION	**WESTERN FRONT: FRANCE AND BELGIUM**

CAMPAIGNS
The Somme 1916/1918, Messines 1916, Ypres 1917, Cambrai 1917, Villers Bretonneaux 1918, Amiens 1918, Bapaume 1918, Hindenburg Line Offensives 1916-1918, Allied Summer-Autumn 1918 Counter Offensive

TYPE: **TANK CREW**

FACTFINDER GUIDE: **WARRIORS**

World War II

MID-20TH CENTURY

RIGHT: PARATROOPERS PREPARE TO INVADE ITALY.

112

WORLD WAR II

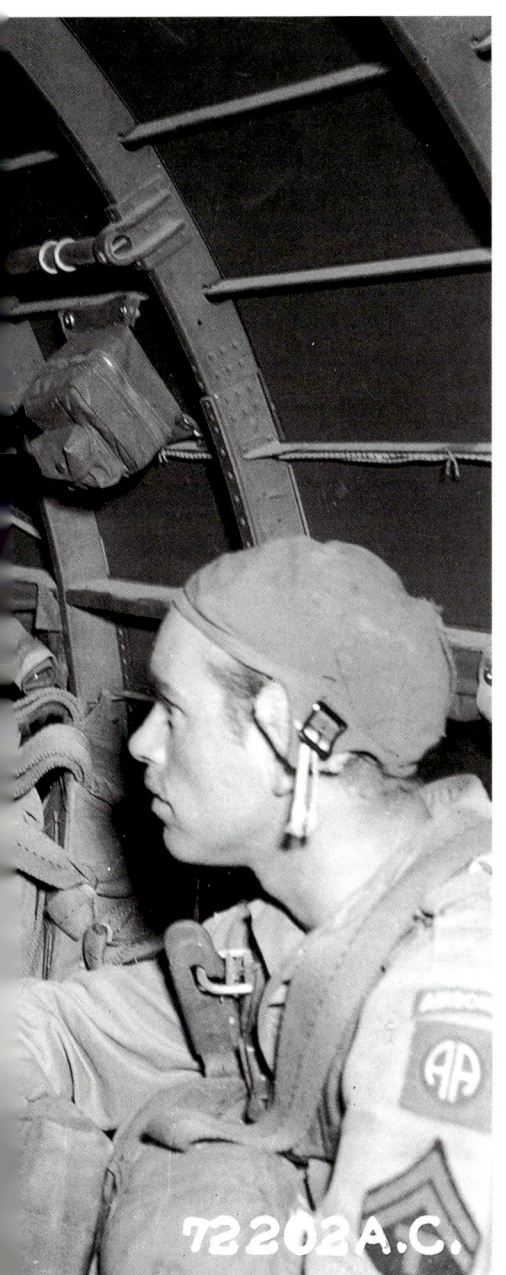

BOTTOM: WEARY AMERICAN SOLDIERS AFTER BATTLE ABOVE: MEMBER OF THE AFRIKA KORPS CONTEMPLATES DEFEAT IN THE DESERT.

FACTFINDER GUIDE: **WARRIORS**

Waffen-SS Soldier

WAFFEN-SS TROOPS POSE IN FRONT OF A U.S. M8 GREYHOUND.

The Waffen-SS (armed "Schutzstaffel" —protective squad) was formed in 1939, from Hitler's elite paramilitary SS bodyguard. The oath of loyalty was to Adolf Hitler himself and by the end of the war the SS had committed appalling atrocities, had been responsible for running concentration camps and carrying out Hitler's extreme views of racial supremacy culminating in genocide, as well as operating as a more conventional fighting force.

The conditions of entry set by Heinrich Himmler, head of the SS, were that the volunteers had to be aged between 17 and 22, be physically fit, look Nordic, and be able to prove Aryan ancestry back to 1750 for officers and 1800 for other ranks. These strict rules were relaxed as war depleted the ranks so that by 1945 Waffen-SS divisions were formed from soldiers all over Europe, even Russia.

The uniform was based on that of the army (gray for infantry, black for motorized vehicle troops, although camouflaged overalls were worn later) with the distinctive SS-runes or other special insignia. Camouflaged clothing was also frequently worn. Officers, NCOs, and tank crews carried a Luger or Walther automatic pistol and the standard rifle for troops was the Mauser K.98. Stick and egg grenades were also carried as were the MP.40 machine pistol or MG.34/MG.42 light machine gun, and heavier weaponry such as self-propelled artillery.

Training was hard, building up physical endurance and mental ruthlessness but there was a strong camaraderie amongst the soldiers. The invasion of Poland in 1939 was the first campaign to see the characteristics of the Waffen-SS in action: fierce fighting, good discipline, and fast movement. Despite high casualties, with the "Wehrmacht" they rapidly crushed Polish resistance. At this stage of the war the Waffen-SS comprised three infantry divisions, but by 1942 each division was motorized, each containing an SS-Panzer regiment. The Panzer tank was one of the most effective weapons of the war, and was important in spearheading the lightning attacks characteristic of the Waffen-SS.

When it came to the largest land campaign in history, the German attack launched in 1941 on Russia known as "Operation Barbarossa," the Waffen-SS played a particularly

WAFFEN-SS SOLDIER

important part in the initial Blitzkrieg that took German forces to the edge of Moscow by the summer of 1942. The ablest commander in the Waffen-SS, SS Oberstgrüppenführer (General) Paul Hausser, had particularly distinguished himself in offensives against Yugoslavia and Russia in 1941.

However, in the long campaign during which the troops were faced with furious defence by the Red Army, the bitter winter conditions (often without adequate warm clothing), and constant partisan attacks, the Waffen-SS also gained a reputation for being particularly effective in suppressing regions where there was partisan activity. Their ruthlessness is demonstrated by their policy of reprisal against whole communities in revenge for attacks by the local resistance. At times whole villages of men, women, and children would be massacred. They also had additional special duties to eradicate the Communist intelligentsia as well as to attempt eventually to exterminate the Slav race, which was perceived as being subhuman.

The three main Waffen-SS divisions that had fought so hard in Russia in 1941-2—the Leibstandarte, Das Reich, and Totenkopf—were reformed as Panzergrenardiers, I SS-Panzer Corps, and the SS was enlarged so that it became virtually a separate army to the Wehrmacht but despite early victories it was knocked back at the tank battle of Kursk in 1943 as the Soviet Army gradually pushed back the German forces.

In Normandy, in 1944, the ability of the Waffen-SS to fight tenaciously was demonstrated by the resistance of the Hitlerjugend Division, which suffered huge losses among its youthful ranks trying to halt overwhelming British and Canadian forces. The end of the war found the SS ranks severely depleted by the years of fighting against increasingly overwhelming forces and at the German surrender the SS was disbanded.

◄ A GERMAN SOLDIER WAITS.

FACT BOX

NATIONALITY ORIGINALLY GERMAN OR GERMANIC PEOPLES, BY THE END OF THE WAR VIRTUALLY ALL NATIONALITIES IN EUROPE WERE REPRESENTED

LOCATION ALL EUROPEAN THEATERS OF WORLD WAR II

CAMPAIGNS
Poland 1939, Holland, Belgium and France 1940, Yugoslavia, Greece 1941-5, Soviet Union, 1941-45, Italy 1943-5, France 1944, Belgium, Holland and Germany, including the Ardennes Offensive 1944-5, Rumania, Hungary, Austria, Poland, eastern Germany 1944-5

TYPE: INFANTRY AND MECHANIZED UNITS

FACTFINDER GUIDE: **WARRIORS**

Afrikakorps Soldier

GENERAL ROMMEL (CENTER) IN THE FIELD.

The Duetsches Afrikakorps (DAK) is synonymous with its great commander, Erwin Rommel, nicknamed the "Desert Fox" because of his elusiveness and ability to live off scraps in a harsh environment. Although only in action for two years—1941-3—the deeds of the German Army in the deserts of North Africa have become legendary.

The environment in which the Afrikakorps fought was hostile. Extremes of heat during the day and cold at night, sandstorms, lack of water, food, and other basic supplies, and the constant danger of disease meant that the army had to be self-sufficient. As the Mediterranean was controlled by the British Royal Navy, Rommel's ability to keep supply lines open or, as with the fall of Tobruk in 1942, use captured supplies was vital.

The DAK soldier was well-equipped for desert warfare. A light olive-colored tropical uniform was worn with a peaked field cap or tan-colored steel helmet. Infantry carried the standard Kar 98k carbine as well as stick and egg grenades, although other firearms such as the MP38/40 machine pistol were also carried, with the Walther P38 pistol being popular with officers.

Rommel's first force in 1941 was fully motorized and included a Panzer regiment. From the start, his characteristic flair for attacking the enemy when weak pushed back the British forces,

AFRIKAKORPS SOLDIER

tired from a long campaign against the Italians. The mobile Panzer tank forces were used to great effect throughout North Africa in massed surprise attacks where the enemy was weakest, supported by the "leichte" (light) division, their superb 88mm flak guns directed against enemy armor, while the Luftwaffe brought in supplies as well as fighting the air war. The Italian Army also contributed to the strength of the Afrikakorps.

Although a continual problem in this mobile war in a large uninhabited terrain was troop exhaustion and lack of supplies, the Afrikakorps kept its morale high, mainly due to the excellent strategy of its leader. A few days before British and American forces landed in Morocco and Algeria in "Operation Torch," planning to trap the Afrikakorps between two fronts, Rommel realized that he needed to arrange an orderly retreat of his forces. The Afrikorps then began its epic controlled retreat from the Egyptian front where they were holding the line at Alam Halfa against Montgomery's 8th Army; the El Alamein offensive then triggering him to attempt to evacuate his army to Europe.

This skilful withdrawal toward Tunisia, with the room for maneuver restricted by geography and overextended supply lines, kept the Afrikakorps out of the reach of the advancing British, while Generals Nehring and Von Arnim held the Allied troops in the mountains, advancing from Algeria. Despite receiving reinforcements in late 1942, including the formidable heavy Tiger tank, and routing the US Army at the Kasserine Pass, an attempt to break the stranglehold of the British at Medenine failed and Rommel was recalled to Germany. The new commander, Von Arnim, could only fight a delaying action and in March 1943 surrendered with a force of 240,000 Axis soldiers.

Under Rommel, the Arikakorps fought a brilliant campaign, but fragile supply lines and the Allies increasing superiority in weaponry as well as American assistance in opening a second front were too much once Montgomery engaged them in a war of attrition at El Alamein.

FACT BOX

NATIONALITY GERMAN
LOCATION NORTH AFRICA: TUNISIA, LIBYA, AND EGYPT

CAMPAIGNS
El Agheila, El Mechili, Halfaya, Sidi Omar, "Operation Crusader," El Duda 1941, Benghazi, Tobruk 1941/2, Gazala, Mersah Matruh, El Alamein, Alam Halfa, "Operation Battleaxe," "Operation Torch" 1942, Sidi bou Zid, Kasserine Pass, Medenine 1943

TYPE: INFANTRY AND MECHANIZED UNITS

FACTFINDER GUIDE: **WARRIORS**

Japanese Infantryman

JAPANESE FORCES LAND ON CHRISTMAS ISLAND.

By the start of the Pacific War of World War II, Japan had already been fighting a war in China since 1937. At first they swept everything before them in southeast Asia, suffering their first defeat on land only in 1943 in Papua. The seemingly invincible infantry moved with speed and surprise, keeping the momentum going in attack after attack, both frontal and flanking.

The Japanese infantryman was feared for his bravery and willingness to sacrifice his life to destroy the enemy. This was the result of a militaristic culture dating back to the samurai warrior and meant that the Japanese did not respect an enemy who surrendered. This would lead to acts of cruelty toward prisoners of war.

The typical Japanese infantryman was a conscripted peasant aged 19-45. The uniform was khaki and included a high-crowned helmet to protect against shrapnel. The weapons had mostly been developed in Japan. The standard rifle was the old-fashioned 6.5mm Meiji 38, although the shorter Meiji 44 carbine with fixed bayonet was popular in the jungle. A variety of sub-machine guns were used: the German 9mm Schmeisser and Steyr-Solothurn and the 8mm Japanese Type 100. Officers and NCOs were generally issued with an 8mm Nambu pistol. Japanese infantry platoons would also contain light machine gun groups and their standard weapon, which accounted for many casualties during the war, was the Type 96 6.5mm

JAPANESE INFANTRYMAN

Nambu. Mortars and grenade launchers were used extensively to support infantry operations. The bayonet was seen as an important weapon and officers carried a heavy sword which they expected to use in close combat following a "Banzai" charge at the enemy. Grenades were also widely used, especially in the jungle.

In the Japanese conquest of Burma in 1942, their superior jungle-fighting techniques and stamina meant that they could operate deep within the jungle, living off the land. Keeping away from the obvious routes, small, independent units of infantry with light artillery would infiltrate British positions using the cover of vegetation, outflanking them, and pushing the British back continuously in close combat. Attacks were often made at night. However, they were affected in the difficult jungle climate by disease and malnutrition due to the difficulty of getting supplies to the troops and large numbers of soldiers were lost.

The Americans feared the high loss of life involved in retaking all the fortified Pacific islands, having experienced the Japanese intention to sacrifice every soldier to maximize enemy losses. In Luzon, in the Philippines, the Japanese army avoided pitched battles against superior American firepower to prolong the fighting in the mountains for a month. At Iwo Jima, a Japanese force of 25,000 inflicted 26,000 casualties on the Americans in five weeks of fighting. In the defence of Okinawa in 1945, Japanese troops defended every yard of the island in 11 weeks of fighting by defending bravely, using the terrain to site strong defensive positions. The Japanese lost 137,000 troops—the entire garrison—while the Americans had 39,000 casualties in the bloodiest fighting of the war in the Pacific. The Japanese army's willingness to fight to the bitter end led to the US decision to end the war swiftly by dropping the atomic bombs at Hiroshima and Nagasaki.

JAPANESE TROOPS LAND IN THE PHILIPPINES.

FACT BOX

NATIONALITY **JAPANESE**
LOCATION **SOUTHEAST ASIA**

CAMPAIGNS
Indochina 1940-1, Hong Kong 1941, Malaya 1941, Philippines 1941-2, British North Borneo, Sarawak, Borneo, Celebes, Amboina 1941-2, Singapore 1942, Guadalcanal 1942-3, Southern Sumatra, Timor and Bali 1942, Java 1942, Burma 1942-5, Battle of Imphal 1944; Guam and Wake 1941, "Operation Cartwheel" 1943, Northern New Guinea 1944, Central Pacific Offensive (US) 1943-4, The Philippines 1944, Iwo Jima 1945, Okinawa 1945

TYPE: **INFANTRY AND MECHANIZED UNITS**

FACTFINDER GUIDE: **WARRIORS**

British Paratrooper

BRITISH PARATROOPERS PREPARE FOR THEIR JUMP.

In June 1940, the British Prime Minister, Winston Churchill, called for airborne forces to be raised, leading to the Parachute Corps' formation. Redesignated the Parachute Regiment in 1942, this was an elite force, recruiting the best soldiers who were given advanced infantry training. Once dropped, the Paratroops often fought on as valued front-line infantry.

The first raid of the newly formed 2nd Parachute Battalion was in February 1942, capturing a German Wuerzburg radar set with its operators from the French coastal village of Bruneval. Airborne forces also spearheaded the D-Day invasion where a parachute and glider force, the 9th Battalion of the Parachute Regiment, seized a German gun battery at Merville, which commanded the British invasion beaches. Vital bridges were also taken by other battalions. Later in 1944, the 1st Airborne Division was dropped at Arnhem in an attempt to finish the war quickly by capturing bridges across the Rhine. The ground-based troops never reached them and despite furious defence of their position the paras suffered heavy losses, 2nd and 3rd Battalions of the Parachute Regiment being virtually wiped out. The lessons were learned in the successful Rhine

BRITISH PARATROOPER

crossing in "Operation Varsity" in March 1945, where the 6th Airborne Division were supported by artillery and ground troops when dropped on the far bank of the Rhine to spearhead the invasion of Germany.

The distinctive maroon berets of the Parachute Regiment were not worn in action, being replaced by the steel helmet. The jumpsuit worn over the battle-dress was called the "Denison smock," designed to keep the parachutist warm during descent but allowing ease of movement on the ground. The parachute was worn on the stomach and there was no reserve parachute. Camouflage was vital: face paint and a face veil were also used. Weapons included the Fairbairn Sykes dagger fastened into the parachute trousers, the rest of the weapons and equipment being carried in a haversack worn on the stomach or a bag attached to the leg. These would consist of the standard infantry .303 Lee-Enfield rifle, or 9mm Sten submachine gun. Officers carried an automatic pistol. Heavier weapons included the .303 Bren light machine gun, the PIAT anti-tank gun and mortars, mines, grenades, explosives sticks, and the heavy Vickers .303in machine gun. The aircraft used for the drops was a version of the American DC-3.

The success of paratroop raids depended on an accurate drop (pathfinders would lead a typical para drop, marking the drop zones for the following aircraft), good weather, complete surprise, fast action, determination to hold onto the objective, and quick support as they were lightly armed. At Bruneval, for example, they were picked up by the Royal Navy as soon as their mission was accomplished. When it went wrong as at Arnhem or the landings in Sicily, paratroops were dropped over a wide area, making it difficult to regroup before they were attacked by the enemy.

A PARATROOPER IN OOSTERBEEK.

FACT BOX

NATIONALITY	**BRITISH, PLUS 1ST CANADIAN PARA BATTALION**
LOCATION	EUROPEAN THEATERS OF WAR, NORTH AFRICA

CAMPAIGNS
Bruneval, Normandy 1942; D-Day, Normandy 1944, Breville, Normandy 1944; Arnhem, Holland 1944; Ardennes campaign 1944-5; the Rhine Crossing 1945, Germany 1945; North Africa 1942-3, Oudna, North Africa 1942, Tamera, North Africa 1943; Italy 1943-4, Primasole Bridge, Sicily 1943; Southern France 1944; Greece 1944-5, Athens 1944

TYPE:	**AIRBORNE INFANTRY**

FACTFINDER GUIDE: **WARRIORS**

U.S. Paratrooper

AMERICAN PARATROOPERS PRIOR TO THE D-DAY INVASION OF FRANCE.

The US 1st Parachute Regiment was created in 1940, followed by several airborne divisions containing highly trained, volunteer parachute troops for special operations. Often they were used to seize vital roads and bridges and hold them for the advancing infantry and armor.

The paratrooper carried as much equipment as possible during the jump. The standard helmet was worn with netting to attach foliage for camouflage (face-camouflage paint was also used). Weapons were the Thompson or lighter M3 "grease gun" sub-machine gun, M1A1 carbine, or more powerful Garand M1 rifle, plus a Colt .45in pistol. Hand grenades, anti-tank mines, and a trench knife were also carried. Additional equipment, such as entrenching tools, as well as personal supplies, completed the heavy and unwieldy personal load for each paratrooper. Additional heavy weapons included bazookas and mortars—these were dropped separately. The US Paratroopers were the only airborne troops during World War II to carry a reserve parachute, although in low drops there would have been no time to open it. They were carried in converted Dakotas—the Douglas C-47.

The US Paratroopers' first taste of action was in North Africa but their value in taking vital enemy positions

U.S. PARATROOPER

and holding off counter attacks in advance of the main force was first shown in the Allied invasion of Sicily in 1943, which was led by the 82nd Airborne Division in a night-drop. Despite a scattered drop, the paratroopers regrouped behind the main landing beaches and pushed inland, holding off a combined German/Italian counter attack. At the Anzio beachhead, when the Allies were attempting to establish themselves on the Italian mainland in 1944, the courage of the US Paratroopers was again demonstrated when, surrounded by superior German armor and without armored support, the 504th held out for 63 days before being withdrawn, having suffered appalling casualties. This lesson that the lightly armed paratroopers had to be quickly supported if their initial surprise attack was to be successful was to be vital throughout the war.

The US Paratroops played a leading role during the Normandy landings on D-Day in 1944. They were dropped low—from about only 500 feet—to achieve maximum surprise, seizing vital roads and bridgeheads ahead of the main force, holding off German counterattacks and neutralizing enemy batteries. They were also highly effective as ground troops and at the Battle of Bastogne, during the Battle of the Bulge 1944-5, they distinguished themselves as among the finest fighters in the US Army.

The Paratroopers also played a vital role in the defeat of Japan in the Pacific War. When General MacArthur's forces were retaking the Philippines in 1945, paratroops from the 503rd Parachute infantry carried out a precision drop from 400 feet on a cliff-top on the Japanese-held garrison on Corregidor Island which controlled Manila Bay. This unorthodox and daring raid took the Japanese by surprise—they had been pounded by an aerial and naval bombardment and were not expecting paratroopers to land—and paved the way for the recapture of the Philippines.

AIRBORNE TROOPS PREPARE FOR LANDINGS IN SICILY.

FACT BOX

NATIONALITY	**AMERICAN**
LOCATION	EUROPEAN THEATERS OF WAR, NORTH AFRICA, SOUTHEAST ASIA 1941-45

CAMPAIGNS
Campaigns: D-Day, Normandy 1944, "Operation Market Garden" 1944, The Ardennes Offensive 1944-5, The Battle of Bastogne 1944, The Rhine Crossing 1945, Germany 1945, North Africa 1942-3, Italy 1943-5, Sicily 1943, Pacific War 1941-5, Corregidor 1945

TYPE: **AIRBORNE INFANTRY**

FACTFINDER GUIDE: **WARRIORS**

U.S. Infantryman

AN AMERICAN SOLDIER, BEARING MACHINEGUN AND AMMO, MOVES THROUGH A FRENCH VILLAGE.

As much as any force, the US infantryman was vital to the Allied victory in World War II. The vast resources of the USA meant that it could put out a huge, well-equipped, and well-organized army of over eight million professional soldiers and conscripted civilians that could overwhelm all obstacles.

The infantryman had to be able to use several weapons, recognize enemy weaponry, and be adept at concealment and patrolling among many other skills. Carrying his personal equipment in a backpack he often had to fight while exhausted and under difficult conditions. It was the infantryman who had to engage the enemy on the ground at close quarters and to hold territory, which meant being in the front line for long periods of time, but by the end of the war the US Army had defeated its enemies with massive concentrations of manpower, overwhelming firepower, and superior material resources.

The uniform developed in the early years of the war, including the famous M1 steel helmet, was extremely practical, with variations according to climate. The highly effective semi-automatic M1 Garand rifle or the lighter M1 carbine with a higher rate of fire, plus bayonet, was largely carried (officers usually carried a .45 Colt or Smith & Wesson pistol), as well as hand-grenades but the development of modern warfare toward using smaller groups of men with a variety of weapons meant that specialist and heavier weapons would also be carried by platoons, such as the bazooka (anti-tank rocket launcher), the .45 Thompson or lighter M3 sub-machine gun, the light .30in or .50in machine gun, mortars, and portable flamethrowers. Rapid movement was aided by jeeps and trucks although the

U.S. INFANTRYMAN

infantryman generally fought and moved on foot.

The US army's two main theaters of war were against the Japanese in Southeast Asia and against the Germans and Italians in Europe after a testing time in North Africa. In the Allied invasion of German-held France on D-Day in 1944, the US Army proved itself in the fierce fighting to establish a foothold on the beaches. On Omaha Beach, the most heavily defended, the 16th Infantry Regiment distinguished itself by forcing its way inland against a hail of enemy fire on the exposed beach despite heavy losses. The fighting that followed in the Normandy countryside was bitter as the "bocage" (hedgerows) meant that the enemy was often hidden but the courage and might of the US Army gradually forced the German Army into retreat. The American pursuit was rapid, typified by General George Patton's Third Army and despite a furious German counter-attack during the Ardennes campaign, known as the Battle of the Bulge, the US infantrymen swept into Germany the next year.

The war against the Japanese was equally fierce as the US Army took island after island, moving toward Japan. Conditions were extremely difficult in the jungle, disease being rife, and the Japanese ferociously defended each position. Casualties were high and progress was slow—the bloodiest battle of the war was at Okinawa in 1945 where the US Army and US Marines suffered 39,000 casualties in 11 weeks of fighting to take the island, killing 137,000 Japanese troops and 100,000 Japanese civilians. The high casualty rate of these battles persuaded the US to finish the war by dropping atomic bombs on Japan, but the US infantry had by then fought with distinction in a variety of theaters of war, bringing the Allies to the verge of complete victory. After its first encounters in North Africa, where the inexperienced US Army had been outfought, the American infantryman had proved himself through hard combat by the end of the war as a tough fighter.

SEARCHING FOR NAZIS IN A BURNING FOREST.

FACT BOX

NATIONALITY	**AMERICAN**
LOCATION	EUROPEAN THEATERS OF WAR, NORTH AFRICA, SOUTHEAST ASIA

CAMPAIGNS
Campaigns: North Africa 1942-3, Sicily 1943, Italy 1943-5, Pacific War 1941-5 including Iwo Jima and Okinawa 1945, D-Day, Normandy, 1944, Belgium, Holland 1944-5, The Ardennes Offensive (the Battle of the Bulge) 1944-5, Germany 1945

TYPE: **INFANTRY**

FACTFINDER GUIDE: **WARRIORS**

B-17 Crew

A BOEING B-17 FLANKED BY ITS CREW.

The B-17 or "Flying Fortress" as it was nicknamed was the mainstay bomber aircraft of the USAAF, being easy to fly and remarkably strong. Although only achieving limited success in the Pacific War it led the USAAF's strategic bombing campaign over occupied Europe against Germany.

This four-engined bomber built by Boeing was newly available at the start of World War II. Developed throughout the war, the definitive B-17G appeared in 1943. It could carry a maximum bomb load of 9,600 lb, had a maximum speed of 300 mph, a service ceiling of 35,000 feet, and a maximum range of 3,750 miles (over 8 hours). It had a crew of 10: pilot, co-pilot, radio operator, navigator, bombardier, tail gunner, two waist gunners, ball-turret gunner, and Sperry dorsal-turret gunner. The positions of the gunners were cramped, claustrophobic, isolated, and (especially the tail gunner) exposed to enemy fire. Armor was considerable, consisting of .30in and .50in twin and single Browning machine guns.

B-17s were usually operated by the USAAF in daylight to enable precision bombing as it was felt that their heavy armor along with their fighter escort could protect them from Luftwaffe interceptors. As the bombers penetrated deeper into Germany later in the war, however, they went beyond the range of the fighters and often had to fly unescorted until long-range escort fighters came into production. In order to further protect themselves the B-17s would fly in close formation: the final development of this was to deploy three-plane elements in a squadron and staggered squadrons within a group. "Lead crews" of the most expert crews were set up to give an accurate bombing marker for following crews, and, later in the war, radar-equipped pathfinder bombers were used to direct the bombing through heavy cloud cover. Even from a high altitude the B-17 could precision bomb—an experienced bombardier could place bombs within 50 feet of the target from 20,000 feet using the Norden bomb sight and taking over the Automatic Flight Control Equipment on the bomb run.

The standard crew uniform consisted of a flying suit, which was often electrically heated for gunners, flying jacket, helmet, trousers and flying boots, and gauntlets, all made from sheepskin to keep warm. Silk gloves were also worn under the gauntlets to prevent frostbite and goggles completed the ensemble. Also worn was a rubber oxygen mask, which contained a radio headset and microphone, inflatable rubber life jacket and parachute—the reserve 'chute was kept nearby.

At first operating from airfields in Britain, later North Africa and Italy, B-17s such as the famous *Memphis Belle* set out to cripple the Axis war industry and military strength through strategic bombing. Daylight flying meant that losses were high from enemy flak and Luftwaffe fighters. During the "Blitz week" attacks on German ports, shipyards, and factories of July 1943, VIII Bomber Command lost 100 aircraft—a third of its strength. In 1943, one aircraft was lost every 11 missions although a tour of duty for the crew was 25 missions, which meant mathematically certain death. Crews had to be carefully selected to cope with stresses of these continual long-range bombing raids so that they could effectively operate the aircraft in the difficult high-altitude conditions in unpressurised cabins. However, despite the high casualty rate of B-17 crews, the losses inflicted on the Luftwaffe meant that the Allies controlled the sky by the end of the war.

FACT BOX

NATIONALITY **AMERICAN**
LOCATION NORTH AFRICA AND SOUTHEAST ASIA, AND OPERATED FROM BRITAIN TO ATTACK GERMANY, ITALY, AND OCCUPIED EUROPE, INCLUDING FRANCE, HOLLAND, BELGIUM, AUSTRIA, RUMANIA, CZECHOSLOVAKIA, HUNGARY, YUGOSLAVIA, NORWAY AND SOVIET UNION; NORTH AFRICA, SOUTHEAST ASIA

CAMPAIGNS
Pacific War 1941-5, North Africa 1942-3, European theater of operations 1942-5

TYPE: **BOMBER CREW**

FACTFINDER GUIDE: **WARRIORS**

P-51 Escort Pilot

A P-51 MUSTANG ESCORT FIGHTER AND (OPPOSITE PAGE) THE PILOT IN THE COCKPIT.

Although early models of the Mustang first saw service in 1940 it was only when the North American P-51III came into action in late 1943 with its powerful Rolls-Royce Merlin engine, that it would provide desperately needed support as a fighter escort for the bombing campaign against the German war effort.

It had a longer range than any other Allied fighter and could act as an escort right into the heart of Germany. The Mustang's fighting capabilities matched those of the Luftwaffe's main fighters at the time: the Me109 and FW190. Previously, the long-range fighters had been twin-engined and lacked the maneuverability of single-engined aircraft, but the P-51 Rolls-Royce Merlin engine's large fuel capacity and the later addition of drop wing fuel tanks meant that the agile Mustang could accompany bombers to Berlin if necessary. The new engine vastly improved the performance of the Mustang, giving the definitive P-51D model a top speed of 437 mph and a rate of climb double that of the early models; it could perform well at high altitude with a ceiling of 41,900 feet and with an extra fuselage tank had a range of over 1,700 miles. It was well-armed with six wing-mounted .50in Browning machine guns.

The P-51 pilot typically wore a leather flying jacket, sheepskin boots, leather helmet incorporating radio, oxygen mask for high altitude flights, gauntlets, goggles, parachute, and Mae West inflatable life jacket. He also carried a Colt .45 pistol and emergency equipment in case he landed behind enemy lines.

Escort duties into Germany tested the pilot's endurance as a mission could last more than seven hours. It required constant concentration to look out for enemy fighters, to stay close to the escorted bombers, to stay out of trouble during the bombing run and avoid being hit by the heavy firepower of the bombers when it was being directed against enemy aircraft. Landing accidents due to tiredness

128

P-51 ESCORT PILOT

were common. The fighter escort had to maintain a cruising speed higher than that of the bombers in order to be ready to engage enemy fighters. This necessitated constant weaving around the airspace near the convoy which used up fuel so P-51 squadrons operated in relays, flying straight to a designated point where they would meet the convoy, relieving the previous escort until being replaced themselves. On the way back home the P-51s flew low, attacking enemy airfields and other targets.

Air combat involved being able to quickly recognize the enemy and good air-to-air gunnery skills. Aircraft flew within the squadron in "finger four" formation, stepped down toward the sun, operating as pairs: the leader and the wingman to protect the tail. The bomber stream would be protected by only about 150 fighters so the escort was often outnumbered by massed attacks by the Luftwaffe.

In the Pacific War the P-51 pilot also had a gruelling role, escorting B-29 Superfortress bombers huge distances across the ocean, often for seven or eight hours, during which they were frequently forced to climb and dive to combat the agile Japanese fighters. The tropical climate was often a danger, aircraft were more unreliable and violent storms could cause aircraft to crash. If an aircraft went down the chances of the pilot surviving were low.

The long-range Mustangs were vital to the success of the long-range bombing missions into Germany. Although the job of the escort pilot was extremely demanding—pilots would be so exhausted they would often have to be helped out of their cockpit at the end of a mission—without them the bomber losses would have been so high as to jeopardize the Allies strategic bombing of the German war industries.

FACT BOX

NATIONALITY USA, ALTHOUGH ALSO FLOWN BY THE RAF AND OTHER ALLIES

LOCATION GERMANY, ITALY, AND OCCUPIED EUROPE, INCLUDING FRANCE, HOLLAND, BELGIUM, AUSTRIA, RUMANIA, CZECHOSLOVAKIA, HUNGARY, YUGOSLAVIA, NORWAY AND SOVIET UNION; NORTH AFRICA, SOUTHEAST ASIA

CAMPAIGNS
European theaters of war 1943-5, North Africa 1943, Pacific War and Southeast Asia 1943-5

TYPE: AIR FORCE PILOT

FACTFINDER GUIDE: **WARRIORS**

Bf 109 Pilot

PLAYFUL CREW MEMBERS NEXT TO THEIR BF 109.

The Messerschmitt Bf109 was the predominant Luftwaffe fighter aircraft of World War II, more than 30,000 seeing action throughout the war.

In the early years of the war it was genuinely superior to Allied fighter aircraft. The Bf109E series fighter had a top speed of 354 mph, a service ceiling of 36,000 feet and was well armed with variants of a hub-firing Oerlikon 20mm machine gun, plus a 7.9mm machine gun in the nose and two 7.9mm machine guns or 20mm cannon in the wings. The Bf109F series that followed maintained the advantage over Allied aircraft, being faster and more maneuverable, and, although its guns were all hub and nose-mounted, the new Mauser 15mm and 20mm cannon had a higher rate of fire and muzzle velocity.

The Bf109 pilot soon became an experienced adversary, playing a vital role in the 1939-40 Blitzkrieg. The aircraft's dominance forced the RAF to continue its bombing campaign on Germany with night attacks after heavy losses in daytime raids, and it outclassed any fighter it came up against in the North African and Soviet Union campaigns.

During the battle of Britain, Bf109 fighter units had several roles: to roam the skies clearing the airspace of RAF fighters, to escort bombers until the fighters could break and engage with attacking RAF fighters, or to fly in close formation with the bombers without pursuing attacking aircraft. Although comparable in performance to the Spitfire and Hurricane (and even superior in some respects) the Bf109 pilot was handicapped by operating at the limits of his range which reduced his effectiveness. By the end of the Battle of Britain, the continual attacks over the relatively long distances flown left the Bf109 pilots exhausted and at the limits of their endurance.

BF 109 PILOT

The pilot sat in a narrow cockpit which was cramped and uncomfortable. Visibility through the canopy and armored windscreen was poor although the pilot was protected by cockpit armor introduced with the Bf109F series in 1940. Tactics involved stalking the enemy, diving from behind and from the sun or cloud cover to shoot them down with a sudden burst of fire.

Against the rugged Allied B-17 and B-24 bombers' powerful defensive firepower when in formation, the tactics had to be revised, causing extra 20mm cannon to be fitted to the Bf109's wings so that more cautious attacks were possible. This reduced the performance of the Luftwaffe fighter, beginning the process by which the BF109 pilot became increasingly unable to take on the new Allied fighters. The BF109 pilot also began to be used as a high-altitude night-fighter, to combat the RAF's bombing campaign. The pilot had to be in a state of constant alertness awaiting the next mission, then scrambling at short notice to race in formation to the enemy bomber stream. Concentration was vital to prevent accidents, especially as the later models of Bf109 could be unstable when loaded with fuel.

Toward the end of the war, the Luftwaffe fighter pilots had to fight to survive against superior forces. The death toll was high—in the first four months of 1944 an estimated 1,000 pilots were lost. These experienced men could not be replaced and morale was low. Fresh young pilots often only survived a few days and the Luftwaffe gradually gave up attempting to take on the Allies. Despite the sterling service that the Bf109 pilots had given the German war effort, by the end they were rarely able to challenge for mastery of the skies.

THE BF 109 CREW IN THE HOT AFRICAN SUN.

FACT BOX

NATIONALITY	**GERMAN, ALTHOUGH THE Bf109 WAS SUPPLIED TO OTHER AIR FORCES SUCH AS FINLAND**
LOCATION	GERMANY, ITALY, BRITAIN AND OCCUPIED EUROPE, INCLUDING POLAND, FRANCE, HOLLAND, BELGIUM, AUSTRIA, RUMANIA, CZECHOSLOVAKIA, HUNGARY, YUGOSLAVIA AND NORWAY; THE SOVIET UNION; NORTH AFRICA

CAMPAIGNS
Poland 1939, France, Holland, Belgium Blitzkrieg 1940, Battle of Britain 1940, North Africa 1941-3, Mediterranean including Crete (1941) 1940-5, Eastern Front 1941-5, Western Europe and Germany 1940-5

TYPE: **AIR FORCE PILOT**

FACTFINDER GUIDE: **WARRIORS**

Spitfire Pilot

The Supermarine Spitfire was one of the most famous aircraft of World War II. Characterized by its superb handling it was a match for any enemy fighter virtually throughout the war.

In the Battle of Britain of 1940, the Spitfire pilot was in the frontline combating the attempted German invasion of Britain. New pilots often had only a few hours of Spitfire flying time under their belt before going into combat and many of these inexperienced men lost their lives. Pilots operated in a state of constant alert, ready to run to their aircraft immediately on the command "scramble." The aircraft would have already been started by the mechanic and the squadron would follow its leader into the air within a minute or two to intercept the next German attack. Other fighters at the airfield would also have to take-off so as not to be destroyed by incoming Luftwaffe bombers. Once in the air the task of the Spitfires and accompanying Hurricanes was to shoot down the incoming bombers, taking on their fighter escort, which was usually the comparable Bf109. At the height of the Battle of Britain, when the Luftwaffe concentrated its forces on an attack on London, the fighters turned the tide, harrying the raiding forces across Southern England then inflicting heavy losses in massed attacks on the edge of London. Hitler was forced to postpone his plans for the invasion of Britain and abandon the daylight bombing campaign.

In the course of the war the Spitfire pilot had many roles: fighter-bomber; bomber escort, and photo-reconnaissance, often at high altitude and unarmed, relying on speed and height to avoid trouble; late variants with pressurised cabins could operate at nearly 50,000 feet.

The Spitfire pilot operated in cramped conditions in the narrow cockpit, constantly on the look-out for enemy attack. Cockpit heating was introduced during the war which improved conditions but electrically-heated clothing was occasionally worn. The pilot generally wore an overall flying suit with parachute, inflatable life-jacket and dinghy in case he ditched in water, leather flying helmet incorporating radio and with

132

SPITFIRE PILOT

an oxygen mask attached for high-altitude flying, plus goggles to reduce glare and protect the eyes if the windscreen was broken. Gauntlets, gloves, and boots completed the kit. In the heat of Southeast Asia much lighter clothing was worn although it was always important to be protected against the dreaded fire in the cockpit if the fuel tank was punctured.

As the war spread the Spitfire became involved in more theaters of action. The Mark IX with its Rolls-Royce Merlin supercharged engine, introduced in 1942, and the later variants with the even more powerful Rolls-Royce Griffon engine were instrumental in the Allies eventual control of the skies. The Mark XIV had an improved rate of climb, top speed of 439 mph, and a service ceiling of 43,000 feet. It was generally armed with two Hispano 20mm cannon and four Browning .303in machine guns. Later variants would give the pilot armor protection and improved visibility with a bubble canopy. A pilot had to be on constant alert to counter enemy attacks, most attacks coming from behind or below, so the latter advance increased the pilot's chances of survival. Late war duties of this versatile aircraft, once the battle against the Luftwaffe had been largely won, included shooting down the V1 flying bombs, or even tipping them down with the wing, and aiding the ground forces as a fighter-bomber.

A PILOT PUTTING ON HIS PARACHUTE.

FACT BOX

NATIONALITY BRITISH; OTHER NATIONALITIES WHICH FLEW THE SPITFIRE INCLUDED USAAF, FREE FRENCH, POLES AND OTHER ALLIED COUNTRIES, PLUS EMPIRE AND DOMINION COUNTRIES

LOCATION GERMANY, ITALY, BRITAIN AND OCCUPIED EUROPE, INCLUDING FRANCE, HOLLAND, BELGIUM, AUSTRIA, RUMANIA, CZECHOSLOVAKIA, HUNGARY, YUGOSLAVIA, NORWAY AND THE SOVIET UNION; NORTH AFRICA, THE MIDDLE EAST, SOUTHEAST ASIA

CAMPAIGNS
France, Holland, Belgium 1939-45, Battle of Britain 1940, North Africa 1941-3, the Mediterranean and Italy 1941-5, including Malta 1942, Germany 1941-5, Southeast Asia 1941-5

TYPE: **AIR FORCE PILOT**

FACTFINDER GUIDE: **WARRIORS**

Lancaster Crew

The Avro Lancaster was the mainstay of RAF Bomber Command. Introduced in 1941, it was a huge advance on the existing RAF heavy bombers. It was versatile and handled easily; with its four Rolls-Royce Merlin engines it had a maximum speed of 270 mph, a service ceiling of 21,500 feet, and a range even when fully laden of 1,160 miles. Up to 14,000 lb of bombs could be carried and it was well armed, generally with .303in Browning machine guns: two in the nose turret, two in the mid-upper turret, and either four or two more powerful .50in Browning machine guns in the tail turret.

The crew consisted of seven men: pilot, flight engineer, bomb aimer/front gunner, navigator, wireless operator, mid-upper gunner, and tail gunner. Conditions on the aircraft were spartan. The tail-gunner's claustrophobic position was the coldest and loneliest. He had to remain vigilant for night fighters throughout the trip—there and back—only able to communicate with the rest of the crew via the intercom. His was also the most dangerous job, being generally first in the firing line of attacking aircraft that could approach unseen at any moment. There was a blind spot underneath the Lancaster that none of its guns could reach—this was a favorite route of attack for Luftwaffe nightfighters which would be concealed against the dark background of the ground.

If the Lancaster's armament could not see off an attacking aircraft, a favored avoidance tactic was for the pilot to corkscrew the large bomber, spoiling the aim of the oncoming nightfighter. Flak was the other great danger as the Lancaster normally dropped its bombs at around 10,000 feet—well within range of the searchlights and anti-aircraft fire. Cloud was always a refuge for the Lancaster but if the aircraft was badly hit it was a struggle for any of the crew members to find their parachute, negotiate passages and jump through narrow exits before the aircraft went out of control.

The Lancaster was involved in some famous special actions. The most famous of these were the destruction of the V-weapon sites and the sinking of the German battleship Tirpitz in 1944, and the low-level raid on the Mohne and Eder dams with bouncing bombs in 1943 by the Dambuster Squadron led by Guy Gibson.

However, the RAF's bombing campaign against Germany was where the Lancaster saw the most action. Despite advances in technology, such as radar bomb aiming and other electronic aids, and in tactics, such as the use of Pathfinder squadrons of Lancasters to mark the bombing area for following aircraft and the use of concentrated bomber streams, it was not possible to bomb at night with pinpoint accuracy. Instead, the policy of saturation bombing was developed, where the intention was to destroy Germany's morale as well as its industrial war effort. Cities such as Hamburg and Dresden were left almost totally destroyed. The long bombing missions, often lasting several hours, tested the endurance of the crew and in 1943-4, before the Luftwaffe gave up control of the skies, losses in some massed raids were 10% or over—a terrible rate of attrition when the average tour of duty for the Lancaster crew was 25 operations. Although the rate of losses eased toward the end of the war, the Lancaster crew, despite the destruction it wreaked on the ground, had to live with a high chance of not returning to base each mission.

FACT BOX

NATIONALITY BRITISH; OTHER NATIONALITIES WHICH FLEW THE LANCASTER INCLUDED POLES AND OTHER ALLIED COUNTRIES, PLUS EMPIRE AND DOMINION COUNTRIES

LOCATION LOCATED IN THE BRITAIN BUT ATTACKED TARGETS IN GERMANY, ITALY AND OCCUPIED EUROPE, INCLUDING FRANCE, HOLLAND, BELGIUM, AUSTRIA, RUMANIA, CZECHOSLOVAKIA, HUNGARY, YUGOSLAVIA, NORWAY AND THE SOVIET UNION; NORTH AFRICA

CAMPAIGNS
Germany, France, Holland, Belgium, Norway, Italy and other European theaters of war 1941-45, North Africa 1941-3, the Mediterranean 1941-5

TYPE: BOMBER CREW

FACTFINDER GUIDE: **WARRIORS**

Ju88 Nightfighter

A NIGHTFIGHTER CREW IN PREPARATION.

The versatile Ju88, although originally built as a twin-engined fast bomber, was well-suited to the nightfighter role, which it adopted with increasing menace during World War II.

The C-series nightfighter versions of the Ju88 were introduced in 1940 to combat the increasing number of nighttime RAF raids. These had fixed forward-firing armament in a solid nose in place of the bomb aiming sight and were often painted to resemble other versions of the aircraft to deceive enemy fighters. Despite the number of Allied aircraft shot down, losses were also high for the nightfighters themselves. Low-speed handling was diffi-cult and by 1943 it was necessary to bring out the G-series. This version had a long endurance, handled well, had a top speed of over 400 mph, and was well-equipped electronically. Armament comprised of four or six MG 20mm 151 cannon: two in the nose and four in the belly, plus a single 13mm MG 131 machine gun in the upper rear for defence. The four-man crew sat together in the cockpit: the pilot at the front of the upper cabin, the engineer/rear gunner and radio operator/lower rear gunner at the back. Later, a radar operator was added to monitor the increasing number of electronic detection devices.

JU88 NIGHTFIGHTER

Advances continued throughout the war: radar and other sensors of enemy aircraft electronic emissions such as the Flensburg and Naxos-Z detectors were fitted from 1942. In 1943, the RAF developed "window," which meant dropping tinfoil to confuse enemy radar into thinking a large force of heavy bombers was somewhere else in the skies, but this innovation was soon overcome by advances in German radar. The nightfighters countered with "schräge Musik" (Jazz), which was upward firing cannon, which came in 1943. The Ju88 could stealthily approach the enemy bomber from below, so that its silhouette could not be seen in the sky, to hang in the blind spot underneath the enemy bomber and fire at its unprotected underbelly, and by 1944 was shooting down large numbers of RAF heavy bombers. The nightfighter could also wait for the bombers to be illuminated by searchlights once they neared their target. Even if the electronic detection equipment was successfully jammed, the pilot could always rely on visual contact. His aircraft's guns were more powerful and effective at a longer range than the heavy bomber armament so, with its superior speed, it had the advantage in attack. However, there were dangers for the Ju88 crew. Often visibility was bad and the nightfighter had to draw close to the bomber to verify its target, bringing itself into range of the bomber's guns. The pilot had to be constantly vigilant to ensure that he made visual contact first.

At first, the new nightfighter was unknown to the RAF and the bombers continued to fly into Germany unaware of the technological advances and new tactics of this deadly foe. On one attempted raid on Nuremberg in 1944 the Ju88s intercepted the bomber stream and shot down 78 aircraft out of the 781 that left England. Arguably, if this aircraft had been developed earlier, and in larger numbers, the domination of the skies by the Allied bomber force and the damage inflicted on the German war effort may never have happened.

FACT BOX

NATIONALITY **GERMAN**
LOCATION **THE Ju88 WAS USED BY THE LUFTWAFFE IN ALL THEATERS OF WAR BUT ITS NIGHTFIGHTER ROLE WAS CONCENTRATED ON GERMANY, ITALY, BRITAIN, AND OCCUPIED EUROPE**

CAMPAIGNS
Germany and neighboring occupied countries 1940-5

TYPE: **AIR FORCE PILOT**

FACTFINDER GUIDE: **WARRIORS**

U-Boat Captain

A U-BOAT RETURNS HOME FROM BATTLE.

German U-boats patrolling the Atlantic almost brought the Allied war effort to its knees in the early years of World War II.

The German occupation of France meant that the U-boats had immediate access to the Atlantic, away from Royal Navy-controlled waters, where they could wage war, trying to break Allied supply lines from the USA. In an attempt to counter the threat, Allied merchant shipping was organized in convoys, escorted by warships but the overall German U-boat commander, Admiral Dönitz, ordered the submarines in wolf packs to attack the convoys in strength, and large-scale battles between convoys and U-boats ensued.

The U-boat was powered by diesel engines. The main weapon was the torpedo although deck guns and anti-aircraft guns were also fitted. The standard workhorse Type VII U-boat had a maximum surface speed of 18 knots and a maximum underwater speed of 8 knots, a maximum operational diving depth of over 300 feet, and a maximum range of over 100 nautical miles submerged, 7,000-13,000 nautical miles on the surface. It was armed with five 21in torpedo tubes and carried 11-14 torpedoes, plus mines, an 88mm deck gun as well as anti-aircraft guns. The crew consisted of a captain, three other officers, and 40 ratings. The quarters were claustrophobic, damp, and filled with fumes; food and water had to be carefully eked out.

Early U-boats were slow under water and preferred to attack on the surface but the Allied breakthrough in breaking the Enigma code and other advances such as radar and concentrated convoy escorts co-ordinated with aircraft, drove the U-boats under

U-BOAT CAPTAIN

water. In response the Germans developed on-board radar and the "schnorkel," allowing them to recharge batteries at periscope depth. Attacks then took place more often with torpedoes at periscope depth although the U-boat was still vulnerable in this position.

In addition to the mass of merchant shipping sunk, U-boats scored some remarkable successes against naval shipping, sinking among others the battleship HMS Royal Oak at Scapa Flow and aircraft carrier HMS Ark Royal. Leading aces were Korvettenkapitän Otto Kretschmer with 44 merchantmen sunk and Wolfgang Lütz with 43.

The U-boat captain could keep his vessel at sea for months, rendezvousing with specialized supply boats for fuel, torpedoes, and other necessities. Precious torpedoes had to be conserved—the captain, who directed the attack through the periscope had to ensure that they were used effectively. Danger came from several sources: aircraft, warships, mines, and enemy submarines. During the attack the captain and the radar operator had to remain vigilant against warship or aircraft attack. Once submerged at depth, on the seabed if possible, silence on the U-boat was vital so as not to be picked up by a warship's Asdic (sonar) which would bring depth charges down on the vessel. Even if picked up by the Asdic, the captain could order a change of depth or a movement of position in an attempt to nullify the depth charges and a deadly game of cat and mouse would ensue.

In the end, however, although more advanced types of U-boats were produced late in the war, superior anti-submarine naval and air power inflicted such heavy losses on the U-boat fleet that the threat almost disappeared. The Germans were unable to regain the initiative and although morale among U-boat crews remained high, an incredible 28,000 men died out of the 40,000 men who served in U-boats.

U-BOAT CAPTAIN LIEUTENANT ROLPH MUTZELBURG.

FACT BOX

NATIONALITY **GERMAN**
LOCATION EVERY MARITIME THEATER OF WAR: THE ATLANTIC, THE MEDITERRANEAN, THE BALTIC, THE NORTH SEA, THE ENGLISH CHANNEL, THE BLACK SEA, THE ARCTIC, THE INDIAN OCEAN AND THE PACIFIC

CAMPAIGNS
The Battle of the Atlantic, the Mediterranean, 1939-45

TYPE: **SUBMARINE CAPTAIN**

139

FACTFINDER GUIDE: **WARRIORS**

German Fallschirmjäger

FALLSCHIRMJÄGER DURING A MEDAL PRESENTATION FOLLOWING THE CAPTURE OF EBEN EMAEL IN HOLLAND.

The Germans were the first to use parachute troops in World War II, having realized their potential for a sudden shock attack before the war.

Airborne forces had been secretly built up by Germany in the 1930s and during the Blitzkrieg attack through the Low Countries in 1940 the "Fallschirmjäger" (parachute troops) were first launched on an unsuspecting world. The heavily fortified and formidably armed fort Eben Emael blocked the route into Belgium. A glider-force of around 80 assault sappers, armed with high explosives to destroy the fort's defences as well as more standard weapons, landed at dawn on top of the fort, with an accompanying parachute force which took and held surrounding road, river, and canal crossings so that the main force could get through. Although the fort was manned by 1,000 Belgian troops, the surprise was total and with the help of the Luftwaffe the fort was held until the small force was relieved by Panzers and infantry the next day.

The next year the Fallschirmjäger were again called on to carry out a daring attack to spearhead a German invasion force. The European mainland, including Greece, was largely occupied by the German forces and the next step was to take the island of Crete to control the Mediterranean. The plan was to maximize the shock effect by landing airborne troops on the three usable airfields and the capital but the Germans underestimated the strength of the Greek and British defences. The first wave of the Parachute Storm Regiment landed at Maleme airfield to find they were expected. In the fierce fighting that followed many Fallschirmjäger were killed before they even got to the ground and within a day the regiment had suffered 1,650 casualties out of the original 2,300-strong force. If the defending Allied forces had pressed home their initial success before the dominant Luftwaffe could bring in reinforcements the invading German forces would probably have been unsuccessful. This demonstrated the danger of using these shock troops, in spite of their courage and resilience, if the element of surprise was lost and if more heavily armed reinforcements could not quickly arrive. Crete was the last major German airborne assault—for the rest of the war the highly trained parachute troops were used primarily as elite ground soldiers.

The standard tactics were to drop Fallschirmjäger from the Ju52 carrier aircraft from 300-400 feet so that the troops would be on the ground in sec-

GERMAN FALLSCHIRMJAGER

onds. The low drop also meant that the troops could regroup quickly as there was less chance of them being dispersed during the drop. Unlike British and US paratroops the technique was to leave the aircraft head first in a diving position automatically deploying the parachute on a static line. The standard weapons of the Fallschirmjäger consisted of flamethrowers, 7.92mm M34 light machine guns, Schmeisser machine pistols developed for close combat for the Fallschirmjäger, and grenades. Additional weapons such as light mortars were also carried. Originally part of the Luftwaffe, blue jump suits with a camouflaged smock and light rimless helmet were worn by the Fallschirmjäger but at Crete the troops had to wear heavy clothing designed for the Norwegian campaign.

The initial success of the first Fallschirmjäger daring attack at Eben Emael changed the make-up of the Allied forces as well as the Germans. Within months the US and British armies had set up their own paratroop forces which were to be equally successful later in the war.

ABOVE AND BELOW: GERMAN PARATROOPERS IN ITALY.

FACT BOX

NATIONALITY **GERMAN**
LOCATION **EUROPEAN THEATERS OF WAR**

CAMPAIGNS
Norway, Holland, Belgium including Eben Emael, France Blitzkrieg 1940, Crete 1941, Soviet Union 1941-5, North Africa 1941-3, Italy 1943-5, France 1944, the Low Countries 1944-5, Germany 1945

TYPE: **PARATROOPERS**

141

FACTFINDER GUIDE: **WARRIORS**

U.S. Marine

US MARINES LAND ON ORANGE BEACH, NEAR DANANG.

The US Marine Corps, nicknamed the "Leathernecks," has a long history of battle honors as the elite, land-based, volunteer force of the US Navy. In World War II its ability to co-ordinate land and sea operations meant that it was ideally suited to spearhead the vital amphibious landings that swung the course of the war toward the Allies.

The Pacific War hardened the Marines to battle, as island garrisons such as Wake attempted to hold off the all-conquering Japanese forces in 1941, before the US reversed the tide at the naval Battle of Midway which included the Marine air force of Brewster F2A-3 Buffalo fighters and Vought SB2U-3 Vindicator dive bombers based on the island of Midway. These near obsolete aircraft were given a torrid time by the Japanese fighters. The second vital US victory of 1942 was the Marine landing at Guadalcanal where the Marines distinguished themselves as tough, disciplined, and well-trained soldiers, beating back a number of heavy Japanese assaults. Temporary Special Raider and Reconnaissance Battalions were formed and landed on the island later in the year to reinforce the 1st US Marine Division. Operating behind enemy lines using hit and run tactics in the jungle the Japanese were driven back, the Marines retaking the island completely early in 1943.

A sequence of islands were retaken from 1942 onwards with US Navy back-up, including the Marine Corps 1st Parachute Regiment's daring landing on the occupied island of Choiseul for a week in 1943 to divert attention away from the forthcoming attack on Bougainville and the bloody storming of the Tarawa Atoll in 1943. These invasions culminated in the Battles of Okinawa and Iwo Jima in 1945. Iwo Jima was the largest all-Marine amphibious operation of World War II although desperate defence of this heavily fortified island by the Japanese cost the Marines heavily. Out of an initial landing force of 71,000, the Marines suffered 23,000 casualties as the 21,000-strong Japanese defensive

142

ABOVE AND BELOW: US MARINES RAISE THE AMERICAN FLAG ON MOUNT SURIBACHI IN IWO JIMA.

force fought to the death over a five-week period.

The Marine Corps uniform was similar to that of the standard US infantry with slight variations in cut. It could be adapted for different climates and in the jungles of Southeast Asia light chino, superseded by olive drab, two-piece clothing was worn with the standard M1 steel helmet. Weapons carried were the standard infantry weapons, including the outstanding .3in M1 Garand semi-automatic rifle which replaced the Springfield used at the beginning of the war, bayonet and hand grenades, plus the Marine trademark Bowie knife.

Although a comparatively small force, the Marines were crucial to US success in the Pacific War, and have provided a model for postwar elite forces worldwide. Their ability to forge an attack at the spearhead of an invasion force, backed up by the Navy, through enemy defences and when under heavy fire when exposed in the water during an amphibious attack, was invaluable.

FACT BOX

NATIONALITY AMERICAN
LOCATION SOUTHEAST ASIA AND THE PACIFIC

CAMPAIGNS
Pacific War 1941-5, including Guadalcanal 1942, Okinawa 1945, Iwo Jima 1945

TYPE: **AMPHIBIOUS INFANTRY**

143

FACTFINDER GUIDE: **WARRIORS**

Royal Marine Commando

ROYAL MARINE COMMANDO TROOPS RETURN TO NEWHAVEN AFTER FIGHTING IN DIEPPE.

In 1940, after the British Expeditionary force had been forced to evacuate mainland Europe at Dunkirk, the British Prime Minister, Winston Churchill, proposed that a force of commandos was set up that could carry the war to the Germans in occupied Europe. These would be highly trained mobile infantry, able to carry out lightening raids on the enemy from amphibious landings, backed up by naval and air forces, to put the German forces on the defensive.

The Commandos' uniform was extremely practical—stealth and ease of movement were vital and camouflage paint and a face veil were often worn. Boots had rubber soles for grip in slippery conditions and also for soundless movement. They were armed with the standard .303in SMLE rifle plus bayonet, grenades, and the superb Fairburn Sykes combat knife, although heavier weapons such as Bren guns and Tommy guns were used.

Drawing from the Royal Marines and the Army, the Royal Marine Commandos carried out a number of daring raids, starting in Norway in 1941 with targets near the coast so that they could evacuate quickly. Their first raid was at Vaagso, backed up by the Royal Navy and RAF and, despite heavy Commando casualties in the fierce street-to-street fighting, the main targets of gun batteries, shipping, and factories were demolished with explosives and a number of prisoners were taken. Several raids followed, includ-

ROYAL MARINE COMMANDO

ing on the Lofoten Islands, Spitsbergen, and Maaloy, and the Germans were worried enough to divert men to Norway to counter a possible Allied invasion and order the death of any captured members of British Special Forces.

In 1942, the raids became bigger. The German naval base of St Nazaire in France was the first target, to prevent U-boats and the German battleship Tirpitz from docking there. The plan was to ram an old destroyer, HMS Campbeltown, packed with explosives into the dock gates, destroying the dock and follow with armed motor launches containing Commando demolition teams to destroy the rest of the dock facilities. Unable to withdraw, virtually all of the Commandos were killed or captured in the heavy German fire, but HMS Campeltown reached the dock gates, to blow up later in the day causing considerable damage to the docks.

Later that year, 1,000 Commandos, with a division of Canadian troops, carried out their largest raid of the war, on the heavily fortified port of Dieppe. This was intended as a dummy run for the future Allied invasion of Europe on D-Day and despite showing great bravery, and the Commandos managing on one flank to silence a battery, the raiding forces suffered huge losses of over half the men during the amphibious landing, many not even reaching the shore. However, lessons were learnt and two years later the Allies were to be better prepared, landing on more remote beaches with specialized landing craft that could overcome beach defences, and again the Commandos would play a vital role, securing the flank of the Allied landings and pushing ahead of the main force to link up with the airborne landings.

Although the Commandos made their name in the daring raids early in the war, they continued to play an important role throughout. Their ability to make surprise lightning amphibious attacks in advance of a main force, such as the crossing of the Rhine into Germany as the spearhead of "Operation Varsity" in 1945, was crucial, creating a bridgehead for the following main Allied armies to enter Germany to finish the war.

DISEMBARKING TROOPS

FACT BOX

NATIONALITY	**BRITISH**
LOCATION	EUROPEAN THEATERS OF WAR, NORTH AFRICA, SOUTHEAST ASIA

CAMPAIGNS
Norway 1941; France 1941-4, including St Nazaire and Dieppe 1942; Italy 1943-5; Low Countries 1944-5, including Walcheren 1944, Antwerp 1944; Burma 1944-5, Germany 1945

TYPE: **AMPHIBIOUS INFANTRY**

FACTFINDER GUIDE: **WARRIORS**

Postwar

LATE 20TH CENTURY

US SOLDIERS TRAINING IN NORTH CAROLINA.

POSTWAR

FACTFINDER GUIDE: **WARRIORS**

U.S. Special Forces

GREEN BERETS IN VIETNAM

The US Army Special Forces, better known as the Green Berets, were formed in 1952 in direct response to the growing fear of the Cold War. Initially, the Special Forces were a small elite concentrating on guerilla training and intended to combat enemy guerillas in the event of a Soviet invasion of Europe, but during the Vietnam War in the 1960s and 1970s the Green Berets expanded, becoming heavily involved in counter-insurgency operations. This involved winning the "hearts and minds" of locals by providing medical assistance and help with agriculture from special camps. Operating in small teams backed up by air divisions the Civilian Irregular Defense Group (CIDG), 1961-71, was one of the US successes of the Vietnam War. Large areas of the Central Vietnamese Highlands were infiltrated by the Special Forces, each village being given military training in conjunction with aid, and within two years large armed forces were patrolling against the Viet Cong. Although ultimately the potential of these additional local forces was not realized they were subsequently used in a number of military operations by US forces.

The Gulf War showed the developing tactics of the Green Berets where, dropped by helicopter in the Iraqi desert, they dug in and provided intelligence and long-range reconnaissance reports. They also used psychological warfare through leaflets and broadcasts to encourage Iraqi troops to surrender.

Training for the Special Forces is rigorous so that the soldier can survive for long periods of time in hostile ter-

U.S. SPECIAL FORCES

ritory with minimal armament and backup. Candidates undergo a rigorous selection procedure and successful entrants emerge after about six months with advanced training in the whole range of infantry tactics, use of explosives, survival, sniping, intelligence, communications, high-altitude parachuting, underwater swimming, and other special skills. Despite their Special Forces background, in the field standard military uniform or civilian clothing is worn in order not to attract attention (although during the Vietnam War a camouflaged uniform was often worn for night or jungle-operations). Weaponry ranges from standard infantry firearms to more specialized weapons: during the Vietnam War a variety of weapons were carried on a wide range of missions,

Following the success of the Green Berets in the Vietnam War other US special forces were set up including MACV—Military Assistance Command Vietnam. MACV specialized in covert operations, assisted by local Vietnamese forces, often working behind enemy lines or in neighboring countries such as Laos to disrupt the enemy, working with resistance groups, retrieving personnel or equipment, sabotaging enemy supplies, waging psychological warfare, and even assassinating or kidnapping key figures. Highly secretive, MACV was also involved in training clandestine forces in Cambodia. Toward the end of the war the MACV force was disbanded.

Additional special forces include Delta Force which specializes in hostage release to counter the rise of world terrorism. Despite the disaster of its first mission, "Operation Eagle Claw" in 1980, to release the US Embassy staff held hostage in Iran, Delta Force has been used with success in later conflicts. Also first formed during the Vietnam War, US Navy SEALS (Sea-Air-Land units) are the most highly trained of all the special forces, specializing in amphibious operations.

A MEMBER OF THE US ARMY SPECIAL FORCES

FACT BOX

NATIONALITY	**AMERICAN**
LOCATION	WESTERN EUROPE, VIETNAM AND SURROUNDING COUNTRIES, GRENADA, PANAMA, KUWAIT AND IRAQ, AND OTHER AREAS OF US MILITARY INVOLVEMENT

CAMPAIGNS
Vietnam War 1961-75, Grenada 1983, Panama 1989, Gulf War 1990-1

TYPE: **SPECIAL FORCES**

FACTFINDER GUIDE: **WARRIORS**

Soviet Spetsnatz

SOVIET SPETSNATZ IN TRAINING.

The Soviet Special Forces, known as "Spetsnatz," were formed when the Cold War was at its height in the late 1950s. There were two wings of the Spetsnatz: KGB Spetsnatz were undercover agents attached to foreign embassies and specialized in political targets, including assassination of hostile regional leaders; the military wing of Spetsnatz consisted of Special Operations Brigades of airborne battalions, many based in the satellite Warsaw Pact countries such as East Germany.

Militarily trained from youth and highly committed to the Soviet cause, the elite Spetsnatz troops were selected for their high level of fitness and ability in foreign languages as well as military skills. They were intended to strike at Nato in the event of a war in Europe. Operating in small groups they were to take out key personnel and attack lines of communication. A crucial target would be Nato's nuclear capacity, which would entail attacks on airfields and naval bases.

In the field, the Spetsnatz wear either standard Soviet airborne uniforms or other uniforms to prevent recognition. The standard firearm is the 5.45 AK-74 assault rifle but other weapons such as the Makarov automatic pistol, light machine guns, grenade launchers, and anti-tank weapons are carried, backed up by light anti-aircraft guns.

Although some of the operations of

150

SOVIET SPETSNATZ

the Spetsnatz have been shrouded in secrecy, they have been called into action in small-scale action in Europe. In 1968, for example, they were used to put down the democracy movement in Czechoslovakia. Flown into Prague under cover they took control of the airport, then assisted by conventional troops made their way into the capital to take the Presidential Palace as well as the broadcasting stations, crushing the attempted revolution.

In 1980, the Spetsnatz were used in Afghanistan together with paratroops, first to spearhead the main Soviet invasion, capturing vital routes, then parachuting into Kabul to capture the airport and crucial nearby air force bases. Within days they had arrested the Afghan government, besieged the Presidential Palace resulting in the death of the president, taken all the broadcasting stations and installed a puppet government. Later in the conflict they were used as an anti-guerilla force, dropped deep in enemy territory by helicopter or aircraft, infiltrating the lines on the ground, ambushing Mujahedin villages and supply routes, assassinating resistance leaders, and directing air strikes. Although the war ended in Soviet retreat, the Spetznaz were effective in countering the Mujahedin in the difficult mountainous terrain, where conventional troops and heavy armament could not effectively function.

With the break-up of the Soviet Union, the Spetsnatz were slimmed down. However, the numerous conflicts between a number of the former Soviet republics meant that many of the former Spetsnatz were used as internal security special forces. The war in Chechnya in 1995 being one instance of the continuing role for Russian special forces. However, the disastrous prolonged attempt to release hostages from the rebel-village of Pervomaiskoye, resulting in the escape of many rebels with the hostages, indicates that with the break up of the USSR, Spetsnatz are searching for a new effective role.

FACT BOX

NATIONALITY	**SOVIET UNION, PREDOMINANTLY THE WESTERN REPUBLICS, PARTICULARLY RUSSIA**
LOCATION	EUROPE, INCLUDING CZECHOSLOVAKIA, AFGHANISTAN, RUSSIA AND FORMER SOVIET REPUBLICS, INCLUDING CHECHNYA

CAMPAIGNS
Czechoslovakia 1968, Afghanistan 1979-89, border conflicts following the breakdown of the former Soviet Union, 1990-

TYPE: **SPECIAL FORCES**

FACTFINDER GUIDE: **WARRIORS**

French Para

FRENCH PARAS WITH 57mm RECOILLESS GUN IN NORTH AFRICA, 1958.

The postwar French airborne forces were divided into three groups: the Metropolitan force consisted of regular troops operating in Europe, the Colonial force was made up of volunteers for overseas service, and the Foreign Legion had its own paratroopers.

The postwar years have seen numerous conflicts around the world to which the French paras have been called in. In the war against the Viet Minh in Indochina, paras were used to complement the patrolling and guarding duties of the regular army to strike at the heart of the enemy, such as in the 1952 airborne and armored raid on factories and ammunition and food dumps at Phu Doan, and the raids on the supply caves at Lang Son and Loc Binh. At the last of these raids the paras had to endure a 48 hour march through the jungle. The final battle of the war, at Dien Bien Phu, although a defeat for the French, was to see courageous resistance from the paras. Dropped deep in Viet Minh territory to set up an air base and force a battle, they were surrounded by a large hostile force of Viet Minh. Under siege for nearly two months before the final surrender, losses were so high that many French Colonial para units had to be built up again from scratch.

The years of warfare that the paras had seen meant that were a highly effective fighting force, developing new tactics, able to go into combat

FRENCH PARA

immediately, and supplied with effective up-to-date equipment, all demonstrated when they were deployed in the Anglo-French attack on Suez in 1956. During the Algerian conflict of the 1950s and 1960s the French paras did not make many drops from aircraft, pioneering instead the use of mass helicopter landings to avoid any losses of men during drops. The paras first saw action in the mountains but were brought in to counter the guerrilla warfare in the city of Algiers, which they did ruthlessly.

A darker episode in the history of the French paras is the attempted coup against Charles de Gaulle by disgruntled French military in 1961, unhappy at the French departure from Algeria. Paras from 14 and 18 RCP (Airborne Regiment) plus the 1st REP (Para-Legionnaires) spearheaded the failed putsch, subsequently being disbanded and incorporated into the 11th Airborne Division.

The French paras have continued to be a vital strike-force. The nature of modern warfare has led the French to set up commando teams in each parachute regiment. These are skilled in High Altitude Low Opening (HALO) and High Altitude High Opening (HAHO) parachuting. HALO allows the parachutist to free fall undetected through enemy radar but requires the parachutist to wear an oxygen mask and be protected against the extreme cold. If the dropping aircraft cannot enter enemy airspace HAHO (High Altitude High Opening) parachuting is used, allowing the parachutist to glide to a drop zone using highly manoeuvrable parachutes. Paras are also trained rigorously to be self-sufficient during deep penetration operations, in which capacity they were deployed during the Gulf War, and have an additional role as pathfinders for larger forces.

FACT BOX

NATIONALITY **FRENCH**
LOCATION INDOCHINA (VIETNAM), ALGERIA, SUEZ (EGYPT), IRAQ AND KUWAIT

CAMPAIGNS
Indochina 1946-54, including the Battle of Dien Bien Phu 1953-4; Algeria 1955-61; Suez 1956, Gulf War 1990-1

TYPE: **SPECIAL FORCES**

FACTFINDER GUIDE: **WARRIORS**

Israeli Tank Commander

ISRAEL'S FARMORED FORCES HAVE SPEARHEADED THEIR BATTLERS AGAINST THE ARABS.

Although the state of Israel was first recognized by the United Nations in 1947, it has remained in a state of military readiness to the present day, having to both defend itself against the surrounding Arab nations and at times attacking the neighboring countries.

Throughout the numerous Arab-Israeli Wars the Israeli Armored Corps has been at the forefront of its country's military achievements. Although during the first Arab-Israeli War of 1948 the mixed-bag of the Israeli army had minimal armor, collected from various countries, it soon developed its tank crews into a professional, highly trained, and well-equipped fighting force, capable of lightning attacks as shown against the Egyptians in the Sinai desert in 1956 under Moshe Dayan's leadership.

Despite usually being numerically outnumbered by its enemies, the Israeli Armored Corps is well equipped and the tank crews have been well led. Israel Tal, who took over as Commander of the Corps in 1964 until 1969, ensured the Tank Corps had reliable equipment and instilled the value of accurate long-range gunnery. Able and aggressive commanders were seen as crucial, and their training encouraged them to take the initiative wherever possible, often leading from the front, ignoring the danger to stand up in the gun turrets during battle for good visibility. (Special protective gear and improved helmets are worn by the tank commanders.) The importance of these principles was shown in Tal's brilliant campaign of the Six Day War

154

ISRAELI TANK COMMANDER

in 1967 as the Tank Corps swept toward the Suez Canal, having lured the numerically superior Egyptian armor away from the main Israeli thrust by a decoy movement.

In 1973, during the Yom Kippur War the outnumbered 7th Armored Brigade held the Golan Heights through courage and superior long-range gunnery against massed Syrian armor and artillery. This remarkable defensive action lasted five days before reserves could reach the brigade, which then launched a counter-attack that drove deep into Syria. Both these wars demonstrated Tal's belief in the value of well-armored tank formations supported only by air power rather than by infantry, in order to create maximum mobility and defend in strength.

Technologically, the Israeli Defence Forces have placed great emphasis on the reliability of their tanks. When they replaced the reliable Shermans with British-made Centurion tanks in the early 1960s the tanks had to be adapted for desert use, and a new 105mm gun added. These more complex machines required the high maintenance standards but provided the precise gunnery demanded by Tal. Following the heavy losses in the first days of the Yom Kippur War, the IDF developed their own main battle tank, the Merkava, which was more heavily armored with a low profile to protect the four-man crew. Weighing 66 tons fully laden, powered by a 900 hp engine and carrying a 105mm gun plus machine guns it was first used in the invasion of Lebanon, 1982. This advanced tank is part of an integrated military strategy, developed to reflect the changing nature of warfare potentially facing Israel, in which tanks combine with infantry, airpower, and artillery.

FACT BOX

NATIONALITY **ISRAELI**
LOCATION **MIDDLE EAST: ISRAEL, EGYPT, LEBANON, SYRIA**

CAMPAIGNS
War of Independence 1948-9, Sinai Campaign 1956, Six-Days War 1967, War of Attrition 1968-70, Yom Kippur War 1973, Invasion of Lebanon 1982

TYPE: **TANK COMMANDER**

FACTFINDER GUIDE: **WARRIORS**

SAS

SPECIAL AIR SERVICE ITRAINING IN THE 1950S.

Founded in 1941 in North Africa as the brainchild of a young lieutenant, David Stirling, to attack enemy airfields and supply lines in hostile territory, the Special Air Service is the secret force of the British Army, used wherever a small but highly trained adaptable force is needed for quick action. Although briefly disbanded after the war, the need for the SAS was soon apparent, and a newly formed unit was to be called into action in a series of colonial wars.

In the 1950s the SAS learned new counter-insurgency and jungle-fighting skills tracking down Communist guerrillas in Malaya. Parachuting into the jungle, the endurance of the SAS enabled them to wear down the guerrillas through continual long-distance patrolling of the jungle. In addition, assistance and protection was given to the local tribes by the SAS in a classic "hearts and minds" operation, isolating the guerrillas from supplies. These skills were to be reinforced in the confrontation in Borneo during the 1960s and now form part of the continuation training of the SAS.

In 1958, the SAS moved from the jungle to the desert of Oman to counter an attempted rebellion. In the final action of the war at the Jebel Akhdar mountain range, a squadron of the SAS, demonstrating the effectiveness of a small but highly trained force in special operations, scaled a sheer mountain at night loaded with weapons to take a rebel stronghold. Once on the plateau the rebels were caught completely by surprise and overcome with ease. Urban counter-terrorism was then learned in the deadly conflict in Aden, the SAS patrolling on the streets dressed as Arabs in operations known as Keeni Meeni, at times using their colleagues in uniform as bait.

The most famous SAS action, which was seen live on television, is the storming of the Iranian embassy in London in 1980 to relieve hostages held by terrorists. Skilled in counter-terrorist tactics the SAS stormed the building at the front and back. Wearing fire-resistant black assault suits and face masks, the windows were blasted open, to be followed by stun grenades and CS gas canisters to disorientate the terrorists. The SAS, armed with laser-sighted Heckler & Koch sub-machine guns backed up with Browning High Power handguns, swept through the building and gunned down the terrorists. One hostage was killed in the operation, the SAS suffered no casualties.

Since then the SAS has continued to carry out a wide range of operations, being involved in counter-terrorism in Northern Ireland, including the controversial killing of an IRA unit suspected of carrying out a bomb attack in Gibraltar in 1988

The SAS also played a vital role in the two recent conventional wars fought by the British. During the Falklands War, 1982, the SAS were landed on the Falkland islands by boat and helicopter to monitor the positions and strength of the Argentine army in advance of the main British force and radio in the information. Airstrips and ammunition dumps were also attacked in deep penetration patrols. The Gulf War saw the SAS continue this role, inserted by helicopter or overland they sabotaged Iraqi communications, identified targets for the US Army's laser-guided bombs, directed A-10 "tank-buster" aircraft to Iraqi armor, and attacked mobile Scud-missile launchers.

The SAS is a classic example of a modern special force. The SAS soldier operates in small units through stealth and has excellent close combat skills. He is superbly fit—selection includes endurance walks—and highly trained in the use of weapons, demolition, parachuting, and diving. But successful operations also depend on unconventional daring action, as the SAS motto states: "Who Dares Wins."

FACT BOX

NATIONALITY	**BRITISH**
LOCATION	WORLD WAR II: NORTH AFRICA AND EUROPEAN THEATERS OF WAR; POSTWAR: MALAYSIA, OMAN, BORNEO, YEMEN, UK AND NORTHERN IRELAND, FALKLAND ISLANDS, KUWAIT, IRAQ

CAMPAIGNS
World War II 1941-5, Malaya 1951-8, Oman 1958-9 and 1970-6, Borneo 1962-6, Aden 1963-7, Northern Ireland 1969-, Iranian Embassy siege, London 1980, Falkland Islands 1982, Gibraltar 1988, Gulf War 1990-1

TYPE: **SPECIAL FORCES**

FACTFINDER GUIDE: **WARRIORS**

French Foreign Legionary

MEN OF 2e REP IN THE BASTILE DAY PARADE, 1978.

The French Foreign Legion has a romantic image with its origins in the 19th century and its early history of its home in the deserts of North Africa. Open to non-French nationals, this elite force is justly famous for toughness, having a rigorous training system, and has played a significant role in most of the conflicts France has been involved in since World War II. Candidates undergo a harsh program of drill, running, assault courses, forced marches up to 35 miles in full kit, weapons training, and experience of combat in winter conditions and mountains before they are accepted. Discipline is also vigorously enforced. To join the elite 2 REP parachute regiment, the recruit also has to pass the para-commando course which includes close-combat skills, jungle training, explosives, and other skills necessary to survive behind enemy lines such as navigation.

Since 1948, the Foreign Legion has included paratroopers who have been increasingly called upon. The first postwar conflict that the Foreign Legion was involved in was the war in Indochina. Despite distinguishing itself in this war, the final battle at Dien Bien Phu saw the Legionnaires suffer huge losses trying to defend a base deep in Viet Minh territory. Beyond the reach of ground support, reinforcements of men, many of whom were killed in the parachute drop, and supplies had to be dropped at night. Battered by heavy artillery and subject to repeated Viet Minh attacks the garrison held out for nearly two months before surrendering. Of the nearly

FRENCH FOREIGN LEGIONARY

11,000-strong original force, 4,000 were dead and few of the captives were to return to France.

Almost immediately afterwards the Foreign Legion was involved in another colonial war, this time in Algeria (with a brief interlude in 1956 at Suez). This constant combat experience meant that the Foreign Legionnaries were tough, battle-hardened troops prepared to engage in revolutionary and psychological guerrilla warfare against the National Liberation Front (FLN) and its potential supporters, first in the mountains then in the streets of Algiers, hunting down FLN units and winning the support of the locals.

The Foreign Legion also acts as a back-up force to French Special Forces. When the French counter-terrorist group GIGN had to storm a bus-load of children held hostage by terrorists in Djibouti in 1976, the Foreign Legion were vital to the success of the operation in holding off Somali border forces.

However, the elite 2 REP parachute regiment of the Foreign Legion has resolved hostage crises itself. In 1978, only two days after the decision to carry out the operation was taken, paras from the 2 REP were dropped on the remote Zairean town of Kolwezi, where they successfully cleared the town and released 2,000 hostages held by rebels. Such quick deployment would not have been possible without such well-trained troops maintained in a state of constant readiness for combat.

The most recent large-scale conflict in which the Foreign Legion served was the Gulf War, being part of the successful ground thrust of coalition forces into Iraq—"Operation Desert Storm" that inflicted huge casualties on the Iraqis. The specialist skills of the Legion are also continually called on for smaller conflicts, being usually the first troops sent in—they are an indispensable component of the modern French military machine.

FACT BOX

NATIONALITY: OPEN TO FRENCH OFFICERS, OTHERWISE COMPRISED OF NON-FRENCH NATIONALS

LOCATION: MIDDLE EAST: ISRAEL, EGYPT, LEBANON, SYRIA

CAMPAIGNS
Indochina 1946-54, including the Battle of DienBien Phu 1953-4; Algeria 1955-61; Suez 1956; Chad 1969, 1978, 1983; Kolwezi, Zaire 1978; Gulf War 1990-1

TYPE: SPECIAL FORCES

ACKNOWLEDGEMENTS

The publisher gratefully acknowledges the assistance of the following in supplying photography for this book:

Bison Picture Library for front cover (bottom right) and pages 2, 4, 52, 53, 56, 57, 64, 65, 68, 69, 70, 71, 72, 73, 82, 83, 106, 107, 108, 109 (top), 113 (top), 115, 117, 120, 121, 128, 129, 131, 138, 139, 140, 141 and 144, 150 and 151;

Salamander Picture Library for front cover (top left and bottom left) and pages 3, 6, 10 (both), 13, 17, 24, 25, 26, 27, 28, 29, 30, 31, 32, 33, 42, 43, 44, 45, 74, 76, 77, 81 (bottom), 84, 85, 86, 87, 94, 95, 96-97, 100, 102, 103, 104, 105, 112-113 (main), 113 (bottom), 114, 116, 118, 119, 122, 124, 125, 126, 127, 130, 132, 133, 136, 137, 142, 143 (both), 146-147, 148 and 149;

C M Dixon for pages 8, 9, 18, 19, 20, 21, 22, 23, 34, 35, 38, 39, 40, 41, 62 and 63;

Military Archive and Research Services, Lincs. for pages 14, 48 (left), 49, 50, 51, 58, 59, 67, 75, 78, 79, 81 (top left and right), 98, 99 and back cover;

R. Scollins; Military Archive and Research Services, Lincs. for front cover (top right) and pages 36, 37, 46, 47 and 80;

Bodleian Library; Military Archive and Research Services, London for page 48 (right);

Dr D Nicolle Collection for pages 54, 55, 60 and 61;

Chris Ellis Collection for pages 66, 154 and 156;

Via Martin Windrow for pages 88 (US Signal Corps), 152 (James Worden) and 158 (SIHLE);

US Signal Corps for page 89;

Arizona State Museum, University of Arizona for pages 90 and 91;

Killie Campbell; Military Archive and Research Services, Lincs. for page 92;

Imperial War Museum for pages 109 (bottom) and 111 (both);

The Tank Museum, Bovington Camp, Dorset for page 110;

US Air Force for page 123;

Jonathan Falconer Collection for page 134;

Colonel G Forty Collection for page 145.